2-9-62

THE SACRAMENT OF FREEDOM

THE *Sacrament* OF *Freedom*

A BOOK ON CONFESSION

JOHN B. SHEERIN, C.S.P.

THE BRUCE PUBLISHING COMPANY • *Milwaukee*

NIHIL OBSTAT:

John Ziegler, C.S.P.

IMPRIMI POTEST:

William A. Michell, C.S.P.
Superior General

NIHIL OBSTAT:

John A. Schulien, S.T.D.
Censor librorum

IMPRIMATUR:

✠ William E. Cousins
Archbishop of Milwaukee
October 11, 1960

Library of Congress Catalog Card Number: 61–8015

MADE IN THE UNITED STATES OF AMERICA

INTRODUCTION

Why describe confession as the sacrament of freedom? Outside the Faith, the word *confession* has overtones of authority, discipline, and perhaps coercion of conscience. To counteract that impression and to explain the true nature of the sacrament, I have written this book. Avoiding technical and theological terminology, I have tried to communicate with the ordinary penitent rather than with the specialist in theology.

"Everyone who commits sin," said our Lord, "is the slave of sin" (Jn. 8:34). My aim has been to show that confession delivers us from the domination of sin. Today we usually think of freedom as political independence or in terms of civil rights, such as freedom of conscience. But these freedoms ultimately derive from freedom of the spirit, and the human spirit is ensnared in sin today. Sin is the ever-present reality. If our theater, art, and literature mirror the American soul, then sin has a strong grip on our people. Some say that the present situation is not quite as bad as it is represented in the lust, perversion, and depravity of our contemporary theater and movies, but the precise degree of our decadence is not in point here. The question is: how are we to be delivered from this oppression?

There is a discernible yearning for deliverance, especially in some of our plays. Underneath the degradation portrayed on stage, one can detect a longing for clean air and blue sky. This search for purity reminds me of John of Salisbury's tribute to liberty in his *Polycraticus:* "Nothing is more glorious than liberty except virtue, that is, if it be right to differentiate liberty from virtue . . . though bondage to a person may seem at times the more miserable slavery, the thralldom of vice is by far the worse. What therefore is more lovable than liberty?"

To the prisoners of their own self-made chains, the Church offers the sacrament of confession. For most men it is the only answer to the problem of their disordered passions. They cannot disentangle themselves. They cannot raise themselves by their own bootstraps. They need the help of a power above nature.

In striking off the chains of sin, the sacramental absolution leaves the penitent subject to temptation but free of the domination of passion. It does not confer a merely negative freedom, however. It gives a freedom *from* sin but a freedom *for* love of God. It infuses a positive freedom into the soul in the person of the Holy Spirit. "The truth shall make you free," said our Lord, and the Holy Spirit does make us free. He gives Himself so completely to the penitent that we can say He becomes the inner law of the penitent. The penitent is not exempted from the external law of the Ten Commandments but he does freely what the Commandments enjoin and he would do it even if there were no Commandments as he has within himself a driving inner law that inclines him to good. In the case of mortal sin, the absolution raises the dead soul to the freedom of spiritual life. In the case of venial sin, it expands the scope of the spontaneous freedom already existing in the soul.

American Catholics do not neglect confession. The long waiting lines in Catholic churches on Saturday afternoons prove that. But we do seem to externalize the sacrament of confession. We seem to consider it an external rite that is partly an auditing of accounts, partly a legal trial. Why so much emphasis on externals?

Since the Reformation, we Catholics have been suspicious of those who talk about "the indwelling Spirit." For many of us the term has a Protestant flavor, probably because Luther lauded the direct inspirations of the Holy Spirit as against the teachings of the visible Church. We have a plethora of popular devotions to saints but devotion to the Holy Spirit is almost unknown among us. We tend to regard as a vague abstraction St. Paul's words, "Where the Spirit of the Lord is, there is freedom" (2 Cor. 3:17). That, I believe, is why we place such a light stress on the work of the Holy Spirit in confession and such a heavy stress on the externals of the sacrament.

But as Rev. David A. O'Connell, O.P., says in his perceptive book on *Christian Liberty:* "If a false Christianity has made the liberty of the Spirit suspect, the evil will not be repaired by a tendency to the opposite extreme which savors of legalism and of the formalism that our Lord Himself found so repellent in His own day." If I have succeeded in helping someone to become more aware of the presence of the Holy Spirit in the sacrament of confession, I will feel that my humble efforts in writing this book have been well worth while.

I wish to thank Virginia Kendall, literary editor of *The Catholic World*, for her work in preparing the manuscript.

JOHN B. SHEERIN, C.S.P.

New York City

CONTENTS

CHAPTER 1

THE REDISCOVERY OF CONFESSION

The Church is very much alive in this second half of the twentieth century. Quite a few self-appointed undertakers in the past century announced that the Church was about to expire. Today the expected corpse is strong and healthy. The vitality of the Church is evident in the extraordinary number of daily communicants, the liturgical revival, the school building programs, the expanding role of the laity in the apostolic work of the Church.

This spirit of renewal is taking a special form in the sacrament of confession. As Scripture says, the wise householder brings forth out of his treasury new things as well as old. Today the Church is not bringing forth a new sacrament, but it is showing how confession answers the special needs of our time. We are living in an age of anguish, of fear and dread of what the H-bomb may do to this planet. The cold war drags on from day to day, nerves become more and more frazzled, men drift into a disturbed state of mind which is a jittery sort of pessimism. The Church speaks to this weary generation as Christ spoke to the people of His time. In confession it offers rest for their souls, a source of light and peace in a critical time.

It is somewhat surprising to see how the non-Catholic world is beginning to find in confession a source of hope it never knew existed. Within the past fifty years (partly due to the growth of psychiatry) the public's concept of confession has changed radically. Outside the Church, confession used to be considered mere disciplinary routine or a humiliating ritual or a small-scale replica of the Spanish Inquisition. Today our contemporaries are beginning to sense what some of them describe as "soul-healing," the same forgiveness of sins which Christ granted to the worried and heavily burdened people of Palestine.

It seems strange that anyone should ever underrate the sacrament of confession. For it has always been a proverb, embedded in the ancient wisdom of the race, that "confession is good for the soul." But the fact is that many Protestants did for long years consider the religious ritual of confession as something sinister and almost scandalous. It was said to be superstitious or demoralizing to tell your sins to a man. Today that attitude is disappearing probably because psychiatry has become so general. For after all, the patient does just that — he tells the psychiatrist what is bothering him, his guilt feelings as well as the dark drives of the unconscious. And while the psychiatrist does not treat them as sins, he does treat them as troubles that are causing harm to the spirit.

Today you will find the confessional in many Anglican churches. Members of the "high church" in the Church of England are quite strong in their belief in the sacrament of confession. Then, too, you will find confession practiced in many Lutheran churches. Luther did not deny the psychological advantages of confessing your sins; he denied that the priest had any special power to forgive. He maintained that forgiveness came through the faith of the penitent, not from the priest. As a result, public and general confession of sins has been customary in Lutheranism for centuries. Yet private confession never entirely disappeared and today you will find confessionals for private confession in some Lutheran churches in America.

Many other Protestant churches are today restoring confession in some form. On March 23, 1959, the Rev. Dr. John

Sutherland Bonnell advocated a Protestant type of confession. Speaking at the Fifth Avenue Presbyterian Church in New York City, he urged Protestant pastors to set up a new type of confessional. This new arrangement would be different from "the traditional type of confessional that has now flourished for some centuries." Undoubtedly the reference to the traditional type was a reference to the Catholic confessional.

In the Protestant type of confessional, according to Dr. Bonnell, the minister will not grant forgiveness but assure the penitent that God will forgive. There will be no atmosphere of secrecy: the minister will be face to face with the penitent. Nor will there be any compulsion about this new type of confession. The penitent will confess because of an inner urge, not because of any law of the Church. In this book, I shall discuss why the Catholic Church teaches that the priest has a power to forgive (rather than a mere power of reassuring the penitent), why confession is secret, why a person in mortal sin must go to confession at least once a year. But the very fact that confession is coming back into Protestantism is a tribute to its worth. As one Protestant churchman described it, confession went out of the Protestant church by the front door at the time of the Reformation, but today it is coming back in through the windows in the form of "soul-clinics," "spiritual-problem clinics," and other devices by which the minister tries to help troubled souls.

The average Catholic is sure that confession is good for the soul but he tends to be rather apathetic about it. He just takes it for granted as he takes for granted the fact that food is good for the body. As a child he probably memorized the catechism chapter on confession, but never really investigated to see how good confession is. It seems a pity that so many of us get so little out of a resource so close to hand. An old-time lecturer used to tell of a man who searched for jewels in faraway countries only to return home to find diamonds in his backyard. Some Catholics are like that. They try all kinds of exotic peace-of-mind treatments if they are mentally disturbed, only to find that these nostrums are useless. All the while their trouble is their sins, but they neglect to take advantage of frequent confession and what's worse, they don't really know how to use confession so as to get maximum benefit from it.

There are a few misconceptions I should like to discuss that prevent some of us from deriving full benefit from our confessions. Someone said that St. Thomas heckled himself all the way through the *Summa*. That is, he first set up objections against his own thesis and then proceeded to prove his thesis. So I will do a bit of heckling of myself from here on.

First, it's often said that confession is dull. For the average Catholic it may be that confession is routine, but that's no reason why it should be dull. The sun rises and sets every day but only a dimwit finds sunrises and sunsets dull. The big-leaguer who is in the baseball lineup everyday, the veteran violinist, the experienced trial lawyer don't find their work dull. If they are creative and enthusiastic, not lacking in imagination, they find each performance a fresh new experience. So, too, with confession. We can make each confession seem different from the last.

One of the reasons why some of us make listless confessions is that we look on confession as a purely legal affair. In fact, I have read pamphlets on confession that gave the impression that the confessional is a courthouse where you pay your spiritual fines. If this is your attitude, then you want to pay the fine for breaking the law and you want to get it over with, the sooner the better. But sin is not an impersonal affair like breaking a traffic rule and you don't repent the way you hand the clerk of the traffic court a few dollars in payment of the fine. Sin is a dramatic conflict between man and God, not between man and a rule book. It is a person-to-person relationship.

In contrast to the violation of an ordinary civil law, there is a deep tragedy in sin. The whole purpose of life is to achieve union with God. We were made to see Him face to face and our hearts are restless till they rest in Him. Every fiber of our being yearns for union with Him — every fiber except that rebellious will, which drives us out of God's friendship and kills our chances for face-to-face vision of God in heaven. The prodigal son left his father's house and went into a far country wasting his substance and living riotously — a good picture of the rebellious will leaving the state of grace. But Christ also left us the picture of the penitent sinner returning to his father's house where he was given a rousing welcome by his father who was elated to have his son back home again. When a penitent returns home to Christ, he is returning to the friendship of a person: he is not making amends to an impersonal code of laws. If the penitent realizes he is dealing with a divine person, I don't see how he can feel that his confession is humdrum or mechanical. On the other hand, I can understand how confession might seem dull if he thinks of it as a legalistic affair.

Confession is primarily and pre-eminently the sacrament of freedom. It enables the sinner to break loose from the grip of guilt. There is, moreover, no force on God's earth that can shake a habit more effectively than the sacrament of confession. Sometimes we think of confession as a tough discipline that has no purpose other than to humiliate the penitent and make him feel uncomfortable. There is humiliation in confession, but not humiliation just for the sake of humiliation. That would be masochism. Rather, it is humiliation for the sake of freedom.

I don't mean freedom to do as you please. Only a very badly instructed Catholic has the notion that absolution clears the way so that you can start sinning all over again. Forgiveness does mean that you are now free to follow your conscience rather than stay tied up in sin, free to be the man

God intended you to be. You are rehabilitated in order to do God's work in the world. You are free to bear witness in joy and liberty.

As Gerald Vann, O.P., says in *The Divine Pity* (Sheed & Ward, p. 101), "The sacrament of penance should make us humble and gay and large-hearted; humble because of the sense of sin, gay because of the renewal of life and freedom, large-hearted because pettiness keeps us isolated from God and self-centered, but the life and the freedom are given us that we may serve God and His family and live in God's love of His family."

I think it is very important for us to rediscover this concept of confession as the sacrament of freedom. Too long have we considered it a discipline and nothing more, something we put up with as a religious duty. It is a discipline, but it's not a whip the Church uses to keep the sheep in line. It's something like the discipline of daily practice that a great musician imposes on himself so that his fingers will freely respond to the inspirations of his mind and heart.

Another objection to confession, advanced occasionally, though seldom with much conviction, is that confession is too negative. The charge is that absolution does not renew or regenerate, it merely erases sins as a teacher might erase errors on a blackboard. This is surely a narrow view of the sacrament. Confession does forgive (and it is Christ who is forgiving by a positive act), but it is more than forgiveness. The penitent who merely wants to have his sins erased cannot have them erased in confession. He must have a firm resolve to quit sin for the future, a determination to amend his life. The sinner leaves the far country where he has been having a wild time but he leaves with the intention of not returning. He has turned his face toward his Father's house and he intends to stay there.

Moreover, it's easy enough to erase mistakes on a blackboard, but for many persons it's not at all easy to erase sins from your memory. Unless you have strong assurance that they have been forgiven, they remain to plague you. Confession does dispel the memory of the sin for the ordinary Catholic so that he can forget it totally. I was intrigued by a passage in Somerset Maugham's *Summing Up* in which he acknowledges this fact: "I have committed follies. I have a sensitive conscience and I have done certain things in my life that I am unable entirely to forget: if I had been fortunate enough to be a Catholic, I could have delivered myself of them at confession and after performing the penance imposed, received absolution and put them out of my mind forever" (Penguin Books, 1938; p. 36). An unexpected tribute to confession from an agnostic!

I do not mean to assert that every Catholic leaves the confessional after absolution with peace of mind. In fact, I think many Catholic writers make a mistake in placing such a strong emphasis on the psychological effects of the sacrament. It is true that normally the penitent will leave the confessional serenely assured that his sin has been forgiven and that a weight has been lifted from his soul. At the same time, there are many Catholics who are suffering, especially in this age of anxiety, from neuroses and their case should be handled by a competent psychiatrist or psychoanalyst. To imagine that a confessor can cure a neurosis by absolution is as fatuous as to imagine he can cure hardening of the arteries. A person suffering from mental ills should see the right doctor.

These cautions aside, it is true that the normal Catholic leaves the confessional with a sense of relief. The anguish has gone and he leaves the confessional a free man. The German writer, Goethe, said after publishing *Sorrows of Werther*: "I felt after having published *Werther*, once more happy and free, and entitled to a new life, as if I had made a general confession." Confession and absolution do give you the feeling that you are now starting a new life, unencumbered with the old sins. For Christ promised: "Come to me all you who labor and are heavily burdened and I will refresh you."

CHAPTER 2

THE MASTER PLAN OF THE SACRAMENT

To appreciate the sacrament of confession, it is helpful to have some degree of understanding of what the Church really is. It is not just an ecclesiastical organization. It is the Mystical Body of Christ, the community of His members who live by His love and who break bread in His name and who believe there is no other name under heaven by which we may be saved. It is a fellowship Christ Himself has established and, since He willed it into existence, the faithful Catholic feels miserable when he is isolated from the life of that society. The sacrament of confession is the means God has appointed for reconciling to Himself members of His community who have strayed into serious sin. Sinners find God and the friendship of God in the Church — in the person of the priest and in union with his brethren. "Where two or three are gathered together in my name, there am I in the midst of them."

Someone has said that confession is the only private sacrament. That is absurd. How can there be a private sacrament in Christ's Mystical Body in which we are all united to Christ and His brethren? The penitent does not break contact with his fellow Catholics when he steps into the privacy of the confessional. He re-establishes a contact broken by sin. He ceases to be a lonely wanderer separated from his brethren and His God. As a member of the Church, he finds the privileges of membership restored to him when he receives absolution.

I think it's very important to have a sense of the Presence that hovers over the confessional. It takes three to make a confession — priest, penitent, and Christ. You can make a valid confession without this awareness but you won't get the maximum benefit out of the sacrament, and there is a real danger that you might make a mechanical confession. The priest, of course, plays a large role in this sacrament. His part must not be minimized. But we have to remember that this is a sacrament that was instituted by Christ, that represents His will for His followers, that was devised to reconcile sinners to His friendship in the Church He established, that derives its ultimate efficacy from His passion and death. That is why I say that His divine presence hovers over the confessional.

I admit it's not the easiest thing in the world for the ordinary Catholic to raise his thoughts to Christ when he prepares for confession. If we lived in a monastery and practiced the art of communing with God, we would seldom find ourselves unaware of His presence. Then each absolution would be simply the latest manifestation of His presence. But to apply St. Paul's phrase to American life today, "our conversation" is not in heaven. The average Catholic is engrossed in business, entertainment, the latest news, and all that is in the back of his mind clamoring for attention. There is said to be a religious revival in the United States today. There may be such a revival in the privacy of the average American's heart but you don't see any sign of it in public life. When the Catholic, therefore, steps into the church for confession on a Saturday, he takes all these secular interests with him. That's why it's hard for him to put himself in the presence of God as he makes ready for his confession.

The ordinary Catholic will probably find a certain degree of indifference to religion in his work-a-day world, but the educated Catholic is likely to encounter stiffer opposition. The philosophy of our time is often agnostic. It is difficult for the educated Catholic to forget what he has been reading in books and viewing in plays, and to raise his mind to God's presence. I am not referring to explicitly irreligious writings but to those books and plays that deal with modern problems, weaving patches of skepticism into the text. Some of our best-known authors strike the theme that God is a clerical fiction, and that religion is an illusion that keeps the masses in line, but whose doctrines insult the intelligence of the enlightened. Unbelief is not as arrogant as it was thirty years ago in America but it still crops up in our literature. Into some of our novels is injected the idea that there is nothing beyond the material world, no hereafter, that man is only a biochemical organism seeking his sensual gratification and trying to survive, that the man who is honest with himself will admit there is nothing after this life and if he is wise, he will give his emotions and vital energies free play, refusing to dam them up behind the taboos and prudery and sober decorum of moral rules from the dead past.

Now the educated man may not be impressed by these shreds and patches of pessimism that he finds in the course of his necessary reading but he will be depressed by all this gloom. When he makes his confession, he has to "snap out of it," change his angle of vision, and see in his mind's eye the living God who loves His people. I don't mean that he has to throw himself into a sort of mystical ecstasy, but he ought to think of the good God who loves sinners enough to die for them.

It was a favorite theme of Marx, and to a degree, of Freud, that God is a tyrant, a fiction that suppresses and represses man. If so, why then did God forgive sins? If the clergy invented God to keep the people in terror and subjection, why didn't they invent a god who would refuse to forgive sins and would pile guilt upon guilt upon them to keep them down?

On the contrary, it is a heart-warming story that the Bible

tells about God's dealings with men. The God of Abraham, Isaac, and Jacob is a living and loving God. He takes a personal interest in every human being. His eye is on the sparrow and His heart is with the lowliest of His children. In this space age, we sometimes lose sight of this personal quality of God's love. When we read about vast interstellar spaces and billions of solar systems in the skies, we admire the divine mind that made the heavenly bodies and that holds them in their courses by virtue of His laws. It's all well and good to admire the soaring intelligence of the divine architect of the universe but we ought not to forget His loving kindness.

Take, for instance, His love for His chosen people, the Jews. He made a "marriage bond" with them whereby they would be His favorite people, but they betrayed Him time after time. Yet He promised He would forgive them if they were sorry. This was certainly good news to a people who tended to think of God as a policeman. He assured them He would not punish them as their sins deserved but would deal with them with compassion and plenteous mercy. And He did convince some of them that their sins had been forgiven. Isaias, for instance, said: "Thou hast delivered my soul that it should not perish. Thou hast cast all my sins behind Thy back."

We would, of course, expect God to pardon His chosen people. For all their multiple disloyalties, they had proved to be uniquely faithful in one respect: surrounded by nations that worshiped many gods, the Jews had preserved the true concept of the One God. But we wouldn't expect Him to show any unusual favors to the pagans. Yet St. Paul tells us that He did forgive pagans who were sorry for their sins. In fact, archaeological records show that all men have had a consciousness of sin and a conviction that God would forgive them if they would try to set themselves right with Him.

Now Christ's principal purpose in coming to this planet

was to free men from their sins. We sometimes imagine He came primarily to establish a Church but again that was only a manifestation of His redeeming function. Reading some of the contemporary references to Christ in newspapers and periodicals, you would think Christ was some kind of "New Dealer" who came to improve the economic conditions of Palestine. Actually He was preoccupied with thoughts of His heavenly Father and with the resolve to atone for those sins that would keep men from union with their heavenly Father.

He spent a good part of His day with sinners, so much time in fact that the Pharisees upbraided Him for mixing with winebibbers and roustabouts. It must have stung the Pharisees to the quick to hear Him say that publicans and sinners would precede them into the kingdom of heaven. Moreover, He forgave sinners frequently, and, as if His own actions were not enough to show God's mercy, He told story after story to illustrate His point, His readiness to forgive. He described the shepherd who searched the hills for the lost sheep and the prodigal son who made a fool of himself, then changed his mind and was welcomed back home by his father. Christ climaxed a lifetime preaching penance by uttering a prayer on the cross: "Father, forgive them for they know not what they do."

Since forgiveness of sin was His goal and chief concern, it would have been strange had He left His Church no special means to carry on His fight against sin. He knew His followers would be plagued by sin down through the centuries. Would He give them no more than He had already given the Jews and pagans?

The New Testament informs us that He did grant to His followers a special device to counteract sin. The power of pardon that He had exercised, He passed on to His Apostles. On Easter Sunday night He startled the Apostles by suddenly appearing in the Upper Room. His first words were: "Peace be to you." These words gave them a hint of the nature of the gift He was about to confer on them, a gift pertaining to peace. Then He breathed on them. This was a symbol that meant He was about to give them a spiritual power; He was breathing into their hearts and minds a spiritual talent. And He said to them:

> "Whose sins you shall forgive, they are forgiven: Whose sins you shall retain, they are retained."

This was a power that involved a responsibility. It was up to the Apostles to decide in each particular case whether they should forgive a sinner or refuse to forgive him on the ground that he was not sorry. But this implied that the sinner would have to confess his sins to the Apostle. How else could the Apostle tell whether or not the sinner was sorry? He was not a mind reader. He would have to judge according to what the sinner would say in the confession.

So, too, today it is necessary for the Catholic to make his confession to the priest if he wishes to be forgiven. For the power given to the first priests has been passed down through the ceremony of Ordination to the priests of today. One of the most dramatic moments of a priest's Ordination is the moment at which the bishop confers upon the newly ordained this power to pardon sins.

There is a certain degree of similarity between this judging process in confession and a trial in a civil court. There is a judge-criminal relationship in the confessional. The priest has a stern responsibility to judge whether the penitent is sorry just as a civil judge has the duty to determine whether the criminal is guilty. As the good judge tries to reconcile the criminal to society so the priest aims to reconcile the penitent to God. In both situations there is evidence, but in the confessional the penitent gives evidence and there are no witnesses; whereas in court, the accused is seldom found giving evidence against himself.

However, the parallel between courtroom and confessional must not be pressed too far. The resemblances are actually rather superficial. The penitent is at the same time accuser and accused, plaintiff and defendant. He is in the confessional not under duress but freely seeking the grace of Christ. Moreover, a legal trial is generally public, whereas a confession is made in private. So while there are certain surface resemblances, they should not be exaggerated. Otherwise we might miss the deeply personal and spiritual character of confession.

It is a rule of the Church that all those who are in mortal sin are bound to go to confession at least once a year. For those who have lost their baptismal innocence, confession is necessary. Those who find it impossible to make their confession should at least have the desire to receive the sacrament. Obviously, if a man is on a desert island with no priest available, the most he can hope for is to have the desire to make his confession.

But why has the Church made this rule about going to confession? Why is it compulsory for those who are in mortal sin? This is a real difficulty for those non-Catholics who approve of confession but who feel it should be voluntary.

Well, if we look closely at the sacrament as Christ instituted it, we can see that He was anxious that the sacrament be used. He was not in the habit of creating sacraments that were useless. Confession is necessary by divine law from the very fact that Christ instituted it. We have to remember that He gave the Church jurisdiction over His followers. He gave it the duty to help its members get to heaven and that duty included a right to interpret the divine law regarding the necessity of confession. So the Church is not unreasonable when it requires Catholics to attend Mass (on Sundays and holydays) nor is it unreasonable when it requires Catholics to make an annual confession when they are in mortal sin. I have discovered that many non-Catholics object to compulsory confession because they don't understand how reasonable the regulation is. One Harvard professor with whom I talked had the impression that a Catholic must go to confession every time he receives Holy Communion.

According to the once-a-year rule, then, the sinner does not have to go to confession immediately after committing his sin but he does have an obligation to receive Communion within the year. He must receive Communion between the first Sunday of Lent and Trinity Sunday. So if he were to make his annual confession and then fall into mortal sin, he would have to make another confession in order to receive Communion within the Easter time.

Besides this rule for annual confession, the Church also says there are certain times when you must make your confession if you are in mortal sin. One instance would be when there is danger of death. A mortal sinner in danger of death must make his confession immediately. Or, if a person knows that he will never have another chance to make his confession, he must make it here and now — if he is in mortal sin. Again, a person in mortal sin must make his confession before he receives Holy Communion. If a person in mortal sin fails to make his annual confession he will not be excommunicated for the neglect nor will he be barred from Christian burial if he dies — but the failure to make his annual confession is an additional mortal sin.

On the other hand, a person who is not in mortal sin might conceivably go for years without making a confession and yet receive daily Communion. For you are never *obliged* to go to confession unless you are in mortal sin. This, however, is a farfetched and theoretical case. In practice, the person in venial sin usually goes to confession at least once a month.

Some Catholics seem to have a vague notion that confession in the early Church was made in public. It is not that they have any yen to publicize their confessions — but somewhere they have picked up the notion that private confession was unknown to the early Christians. The error arises from confusing confession with public penance. The public penances in those early days were stiff and not uncommon. Yet they were restricted to notorious sinners whose sin was known to the public and who had lived in arrogant defiance of Christian laws. The confession preceding the imposition of the public penance was, however, made in secret. Pope Leo the Great reprimanded certain bishops for permitting confessions to be read publicly and asserted that such a practice was against the Apostolic rule. "The sins that burden the conscience are to be revealed to priests only, and in secret confession." I feel sure that if Catholics were polled on the privacy of confession, they would vote for it unanimously. The normal human being has no desire to publicize his sins.

The Code of Canon Law contains some special legislation regarding confessors for members of religious orders, but lay persons may make their confessions to any authorized priest. You are under no obligation, therefore, to go to your own parish church for confession. You are perfectly free to choose any confessor you prefer. This is but one of many examples of the Church's unremitting effort to secure for the faithful a serene liberty of conscience.

CHAPTER 3

FORGIVENESS OF VENIAL SINS

Neither Christ nor His Church requires us to confess venial sins. I can picture some fair lady parishioner aghast at such an idea or a professional bigot chuckling over this evidence of moral laxity in the Roman Church, the Scarlet Woman. The Church, however, is not minimizing venial sins nor relaxing her age-old standards when she says that you are perfectly free to confess or not confess venial sins. She has never made confession of these sins compulsory and she has good reason for this policy.

First, to get a better understanding of what venial sin is, let us take a look at what it is not – mortal sin. It will have to be a very inadequate look, for who can possibly penetrate into the mystery of the malice that is present in mortal sin? It is defined as a violation of a moral law in a serious matter with sufficient reflection and full consent of the will. If the matter is not a serious one, or if the sinner is not sufficiently aware of what he is doing, or if aware, does not give full consent, then the sin is not mortal. Picturesque similes and metaphors may help the imagination to arrive at some concept of the essential evil in mortal sin but they don't really get you very far. Preachers may make your hair stand on end by comparing mortal sin to the atrocities of a Nazi concentration camp or the ravages of cancer or the putrid corruption of fruit. But you have to remember that no illustrations of mortal sin are adequate, no matter how vivid, for sin is not visible or tangible and no pictures can begin to suggest the enormity of an offense against the living God. Mortal sin is an insult to the infinite goodness of God who is deserving of infinite honor and at the same time it devastates the soul by killing the divine life that God gave the soul at baptism.

In contrast to mortal sin, venial sin is only a minor spiritual ailment. It is one thing to die and something else again to have a mere cold in the head. I don't mean to belittle venial sin. It would be a grave mistake to dismiss it as a mere trifle. Cardinal Newman was restating the ancient teaching of the Church when he wrote that a venial sin is a greater metaphysical evil than a global catastrophe that would bring death to millions. The mind of the Church is that moral evil, being an offense against the infinite God, is worse than any physical harm that might happen to men. It's hard for us ordinary human beings to realize this but the martyrs did, and they were ready to undergo certain terrible punishments rather than commit even the slightest venial sin.

However, the word *venial* means "easily pardonable" and that brings us to the heart of the matter. Venial sins can of course be pardoned in confession but since they are easily pardonable, they can also be pardoned in other ways than in confession. For instance, you can have your venial sins forgiven by receiving Communion. Therefore, since venial sins can be remitted through other channels, the Church teaches that you are under no compulsion to confess them in the confessional. This means that a person who has only venial sins on his soul can go to confession with a sense of complete and perfect freedom because he knows that he is not obliged to confess these sins.

When you confess venial sins, your purpose is entirely different from your purpose in confessing mortal sins. To use a consecrated expression, your aim is spiritual progress. You confess mortal sins to rejoin the family of God, from which you have become an outcast. You want to share again with Christ our Brother in the rich life of the family of the Blessed Trinity. You turn your back on mortal sin as the prodigal son turned his back on the far country where "he wasted his substance living riotously" and you direct your steps homeward in the hope of being re-established in the family. But when you have only venial sins on your soul, your aim is quite different. As Monsignor Knox said somewhere in his writings, you are still in your Father's house when you are in venial sin but you are looking out the windows and perhaps wishing yourself back in the gutter. Or to phrase it another way, your aim in confessing your venial sins is not to be restored to the good graces of the family of God but to become a better member of the family and to grow in grace.

In the early Christian centuries, the faithful did not confess their venial sins. They knew there were other ways of having sins forgiven. At a later date, monks in monasteries started the practice of confessing venial sins and found it a very helpful practice. From the monasteries the practice spread to the laity.[1] No church law, however, was ever passed requiring the faithful to confess venial sins. It is true there is a law that a person in mortal sin must go to confession at least once a year but obviously that applies only to persons in mortal sin. There have been some theologians who claimed that a penitent should present himself to a confessor once a year, regardless of the state of his soul, but most theologians reject such a suggestion.

Like frequent Communion, frequent confession of venial sins is a very effective means of making spiritual advancement, and like frequent Communion, it is not compulsory. It was precisely because the monks found it so helpful that the practice spread to the laity. Pope Pius VI termed "pernicious" the proposition that the faithful should not confess

[1] Rev. Ph. Scharsch, O.M.I., *Confession As a Means of Spiritual Progress* (St. Louis: Herder, 1930), p. 42.

venial sins at all. He asserted that such a notion was opposed to the practice of the saints and faithful Christians, as approved by the Council of Trent. In recent centuries, therefore, the Church has warmly recommended the practice. Pope Pius XII, in his Encyclical on the Mystical Body (1943), deplored as "disastrous" the efforts of certain young priests who opposed frequent confession of venial sins.

The next logical question is: why has the Church recommended the practice of confessing venial sins over these other ways of receiving forgiveness for sins? In general the reason is that the other methods work indirectly while the sacramental power and interior contrition in confession are aimed directly at sin and more effectively destroy it. True, baptism and extreme unction do forgive sins directly but the first can be administered only once in a lifetime and the second only in danger of death. The other ordinary methods of forgiving venial sins, however, are not designed specifically to pardon sins. With them, pardon is a by-product.

What are these other methods of forgiving venial sins? The Council of Trent tells us that Holy Eucharist can free us from our daily trespasses. It produces charity and charity covers a multitude of sins. The Eucharist, the food of angels, is medicine for spiritual ills. "Behold the Lamb of God," says the priest just before distributing Communion at Mass, "behold Him Who takes away the sins of the world." Then, too, other sacraments such as confirmation, holy orders, and matrimony possess a cleansing power even though they were not instituted for this specific purpose. The Mass induces sorrow for sin in those who offer it worthily with the priest, and this sorrow pardons venial sins.

The symbols blessed by the Church confer a grace which strengthens desires and acts of virtue and these desires in turn destroy venial sin. Holy water taken on entering a church symbolizes a desire to be cleansed from sin and this desire produces in the penitent a spirit that forgives light sins. There is an old and very true maxim that almsgiving extinguishes sin as water extinguishes fire. In fact, any good work, done with a penitential purpose, can forgive venial sins. The methods mentioned forgive venial sins but of course they produce their effect only indirectly. Confession, on the contrary, remits venial sins directly.

There is still another reason why the Church recommends the confessing of these light sins: the words of absolution spoken by the priest give the penitent a greater psychological assurance of forgiveness than do these other methods. Yes, I can have my venial sins forgiven by donating something to the poor, provided I have the right motives; but after I have given the alms, I will probably begin to worry about my motives. Did I have a deduction on my income tax at the back of my mind when I thought I was being generous? Or did I give a beggar a quarter just to be rid of him, or did I give a substantial charity donation hoping to get my name on a publicized list of donors? When you *confess* your venial sins, however, you have no reason to worry. You hear the words of absolution and you are sure your sins are forgiven.

In short, confession is the most effective way of having venial sins forgiven. You are not going around Robin Hood's barn; you are aiming straight at the target of sin. Your sorrow is much more deliberate and intense than in the other methods of forgiveness such as almsgiving or the use of sacramentals. Your contrition is not vague but is a decisive act of the will by which you detest sin because of its deformity. If you are really serious about making spiritual progress, you can find no acceptable substitute for regular confession of venial sins. It is the shortest and quickest path to your goal.

Perhaps you wonder why I stress the fact that there is no law requiring you to confess venial sins. The reason is that you ought to feel perfectly free in making your confession of light sins. If you are tense and nervous in the confession, you won't receive the maximum benefit of the sacrament. But if you know there is no compulsion about confessing your venial sins, you can feel perfectly free and at ease in telling them. Devout converts are often jittery when preparing for confession the first few times after baptism and they find it a rather frightening experience. It is to them especially that the Church says: "You are doing this voluntarily, so go freely, serenely and without any anxiety."

Since they are not compelled to confess light sins, some people wait until they "feel" like going to confession. But this is not a very intelligent way to approach a matter that deserves thoughtful consideration. You can't wait for your glands to perk you up before you decide to make a confession. They are too unpredictable; they make you feel like a million dollars one day and like a dishrag the next, but being utterly oblivious of sin, those glands may neglect for months to whip up that breathless craving for confession. When God holds out to you an opportunity to come closer to Him in the sacrament of penance, don't pass up the opportunity simply because your emotions at the moment have a low voltage. Grasp the inspiration of grace lest it pass you by.

On the other hand, you do have to beware of making your regular confession in a mechanical fashion. Put your heart into it. There is a little devil that can take all the glow and enthusiasm out of your confession and make it seem like dry-as-dust drudgery. He usually starts off by insisting that you draw up a meticulous list of your venial sins. What could be duller than a detailed catalogue of your past errors? Focus your attention mainly on the future. That's far more interesting than the dead past. The past is prologue, as Shakespeare said, but in the confessional you ought to be looking to the future as the purpose of amendment is at the heart and core of a good confession. This question of painfully mathematical confessions, however, is something I will leave for discussion in the chapter on the examination of conscience.

Some penitents are constantly worried about their venial sins. They think these small sins are evidence of a fundamental disloyalty to Christ. They imagine that if they were really making a serious effort, they wouldn't have anything to confess but would come to confession with a clean slate. Cardinal Newman has written something that I think should be encouraging to such disgruntled souls: "Do you believe and act on this belief, that His light penetrates and shines through your heart as the sun's beams through a room? You know how things look when the sun's beams are on it — the very air then appears full of impurities which, before it came out, were not seen. So it is with our souls. We are full of stains and corruptions, we see them not, they are like the air before the sun shines; but though we see them not, God sees them: He pervades us as the sunbeam."[2] If God sees your sins and is patient with them, why should you be discouraged? And if God lights up the soul to let you see your sins, you ought to be happy that you are able to see what He illuminates. You would have reason to worry if you were spiritually blind and incapable of discerning the impurities within you.

Can you be happy about venial sins? No, but you can be happy about the opportunity to confess them. This may seem pietistic. Someone may say that you ought to feel downright cheap and miserable in having to admit you sinned, and that feeling glad about going to confession is a perverted form of piety. But confessing venial sins is a means of self-improvement, and what is so repulsive about self-improve-

[2] *Selections From the Parochial and Plain Sermons:* "Sincerity and Hypocrisy," by John Henry Newman (New York: Longmans, Green, 1908), p. 95.

ment? Does the golfer wear a long face when he practices to improve his game? Must the sand lotter have the blues when he develops his batting stance? Should the housewife feel depressed when she dresses up for a special occasion?

I admit a great many devout Catholics do feel slightly glum and uncomfortable when they make their confession of venial sins. Yet I think it's wrong and that it derives mainly from an excessive fear of God rather than from the love of God which is characteristically Catholic. The author of *The Imitation of Christ* says that nothing is sweeter or better or happier than love, and that one who loves God is merry in God, runs swiftly and is free in soul. One very proper Anglo-Saxon writer referred to "the cafeteria atmosphere" in a church in Italy when she was describing the informal behavior of the peasant worshipers. Accustomed to the frigid decorum of fashionable churches, she considered the simple devotion of these worshipers as vulgar. She was not used to seeing real devotion in action. It reminds me of the Negro woman who stepped into a church for the fashionable set one Sunday morning in New York. During the ministerial service, she began to praise the Lord in very audible tones. When the usher threatened to expel her, she explained she was only praising the Lord. The usher replied: "Madam, that is not done in this church."

If you really love God and have confidence in Him, you feel free in His sacramental presence. To be without Him is the pain of hell but as *The Imitation of Christ* has it, to be with Him is paradise. Did Mary Magdalene or St. John or Lazarus feel uncomfortable in His presence? Tertullian, the early Christian writer, thought of the relationship between God and man as the relationship of master to slave, but Tertullian left the Church as a heretic. Later on there were other writers who claimed St. Augustine as their authority and they wrote in a pessimistic strain. They pictured human nature as a cesspool of corruption despised by God.

Michael Muller, in his *St. Francis de Sales*,[3] quotes one of these writers: "Woe is me. I am a putrefying corpse, the food for worms, a dirty vessel, the food for fire." That's a pleasant thought calculated to inspire a man to great achievements! Muller points out that this bilious and lugubrious attitude about human nature derives from a lack of confidence in and love of God. The pessimist ignores God's generous gifts to the soul, pays no attention to the indwelling Guest and focuses all his attention on his own shortcomings. He is like a visitor to the White House who might busy himself removing chewing gum from the sole of his shoe while the President of the United States was talking to him.

This pessimistic attitude looks like humility, but it's not the real thing. In the properly balanced spiritual life there must be a blend of humility and confidence in God, an awareness of human weakness, but at the same time a confidence that you can do all things in God who strengthens you. If you put all the emphasis on humility, then your spiritual life becomes a lopsided thing. You begin to imagine that it's somewhat indecent to be cheerful. You feel that any kind of fun is secular and to be avoided, or else you become so grimly puritanical that you consider all joy sinful. This is an attitude that certainly cannot be reconciled with Christ's frequent allusions to joy such as: "Your heart shall rejoice and your joy no one shall take from you."

St. Thomas Aquinas condemned this pessimistic frame of mind. He said that such is not humility at all but essentially ungratefulness to God. St. Francis de Sales echoed St. Thomas and said that we must remember God's gifts as well as our sins. Ultimately, I suppose, this whole matter of religious attitude goes back to our concept of God. Some of us somewhere along the line of our religious education acquired the notion that God is a plug-ugly policeman with a nasty

---

[3] Michael Muller, St. Francis de Sales (New York: Sheed & Ward, 1937), p. 66.

disposition. Such a notion makes us shudder every time we think of our offenses against the tyrant. But if we have the right idea of God, if we have been taught to think of Him as our Father, as the Lord's Prayer teaches us to think of Him, then we will see ourselves as children whom the Father is only too ready to forgive. Coventry Patmore dramatizes this attitude in his poem, *Toys*. In the poem a father punishes his son for disobedience and puts him to bed. Later he goes to the bedside of the child to find he has fallen asleep after playing with his toys to assuage his grief. The father kisses away the child's tears, leaving others of his own. Then he muses on the fact that just as he has pardoned his own son, for his juvenile offenses, so the heavenly Father will forgive men their childishness.

What practical difference does all this make as far as confession is concerned? It makes this very important difference. If you think you are a worm and no man, you will find no inspiration, no encouragement, no incentive to spiritual progress. You will have a worm's-eye view of the whole spiritual life. You will ignore your spiritual talents and bury them under a false humility. When you confess your venial sins, you will do so grudgingly, without love, and with a panicky fear of a stern God who demands an eye for an eye.

Christian optimism, on the other hand, is no new fad. In his book on St. Francis de Sales, Muller outlines a short history of Christian optimism. He shows how the desert fathers considered sadness an evidence of the presence of evil spirits. The early Christians had an original list of eight capital sins instead of seven as we have at present, and the list included sadness as a real source of sin. Anyone who allowed himself to fall prey to sadness was given a penance as for avarice or other sins. St. Francis of Assisi reaffirmed this earlier teaching and used to refer to sadness as a disease. He considered joy a defense against the devil.

The sin that we now list as *sloth* in our catechisms was

described by St. Thomas as a feeling of melancholy sluggishness in the pursuit of some spiritual good we have a duty to achieve. Sometimes it has been called *acedia,* from the Greek word which means a feeling of "not caring." It indicates a sense of being "fed up" with the spiritual life, a spiritual torpor or apathy. I suppose everyone at some time or other has been tempted to give way to a glum, heavy tedium when he thinks of the struggle of living a good spiritual life in the midst of people who love a soft life and sneer at any kind of self-discipline. First Satan takes us down in the dumps with the question: "Is it all worthwhile?" Then he urges us to settle back into a listless, devil-may-care ennui in which we begin to indulge in a little self-sympathy. This insipid mood, and the long face that usually goes with it, are utterly opposed to the whole spirit of the First Commandment: "Thou shalt love the Lord thy God with thy whole heart, and with thy whole soul, and with thy whole strength, and with all thy mind."

At any rate, the confessional is no place for sadness. Before beginning your examination of conscience, since joy is one of the fruits of the Holy Spirit, ask the Holy Spirit for help in dispelling this sadness. Even if you have slipped badly and have a long list of venial sins, don't give in. You will be tempted to imagine your sadness comes from humility but it probably comes from disappointed pride. Your pride is irked by your failure to avoid sin. Even if you have a natural bent toward melancholy, chase away the sad-eyed wolf that comes to you in the sheep's clothing of humility. Suppose you do have a long list of venial sins: God will not be surprised or scandalized. He will, however, be disappointed if you make no attempt to get rid of your black moods.

You will find a Christian sense of humor invaluable in making spiritual progress. I realize there is a tendency in certain Catholic circles today to belittle humor as a coy form of escapism from the troubles of our time. We are told that the modern crisis is too grim for jokes and that every man should be personally involved in the anguish of our era. However, I don't mean wit when I speak of a Christian sense of humor. Wit is often caustic and can knife you with a casual quip. Wit is the product of a quick mind and a nimble tongue and often bears no relation whatever to spiritual optimism.

By a Christian sense of humor I mean a Christian sense of proportion by which you see all things that happen to you from the perspective of eternity. "What doth it profit a man if he gain the whole world and suffer the loss of his own soul?" With your eyes fixed on your final goal, the good things God has stored up for those who love Him, you can form a right mental attitude toward the daily events that seem so everlastingly important when they happen but which are actually of little lasting significance. Without a sense of humor, you apply your own petty standards which magnify trifles into mountains of trouble.

St. Teresa of Avila said: "Let nothing disturb thee, nothing affright thee, all things are passing, God never changes." That is true, but I don't think it is the full truth. I don't see how we can avoid being disturbed at times, and so I would phrase it: "Let no disturbance disturb thee. . . ." Some persons claim they postpone confession because they are in such mental distress that they simply cannot make a good confession. Others may not stay away from regular confession but they do allow inner storms to confuse and bewilder them at the time of confession. In the ordinary case, a person with a Christian sense of humor will take a mental or emotional disturbance in stride. His humor is the balance wheel that enables him to get through this temporal world without losing the eternal things. I say "in the ordinary case," for if there is a really serious mental condition, the penitent ought to see a good psychiatrist.

The normal person, however, need not be upset by certain

apparently neurotic symptoms. If any one of us is put under great pressure, the strain may begin to show up in the form of neurotic symptoms. If your nervous system is especially sensitive, a slight pressure or unusual tension may precipitate a neurosis. Conversely, the more normal your nervous system, the greater the pressure needed to create a disturbance.

In short, you tend to show neurotic symptoms when you are undergoing great strain. That is natural. For instance, the psychiatrist will say that a highly sensitive person under strain will probably become irritable, perspire freely, lose his appetite and fall back on various devices to protect his ego. He may try to rationalize some act he did from a purely emotional reason, or he may unconsciously put the blame for his own act on the shoulders of someone else. All this is to be expected. Being an editor myself, I know how unbearable editors can become as the deadline nears. Churchill said of General Montgomery that he was incomparable in defeat, insufferable in victory. I suppose most editors are insufferable when they are in the throes of writing an editorial. At any rate, there is some psychic fear, some sense of inadequacy and insecurity that most of us experience at some time or other. Usually it plays hob with our mental equilibrium for a time but the important thing is to swing back into stride as soon as possible. And even when you are in the middle of one of these states, don't stay away from your regular confession. Your distress is not necessarily a sign that you are deteriorating mentally or that you are reverting to your childhood. Your psyche has simply been "acting up" because it has been under pressure.

Possibly you experience a continuing subconscious sense of guilt that is painful. It may be due to a false concept of a harsh God you have developed over the years. If you are an adult, it may be too late for you to change this subconscious relationship to God but at least you can learn to live with it. You can challenge it. If you feel guilty even though you know you are not guilty, use your intelligence to say, "I'm not responsible for this. This is an emotion." Or you might say, "I *feel* guilty but I know I'm not guilty, so what?" By facing up to the compulsion, you can at least dull the force of it even if you can't get rid of it entirely. These permanent tensions are, of course, harder to handle than temporary ones but they can be controlled to a certain degree by intelligent treatment.

Great saints have undergone disturbing mental states in which they felt that God was abandoning them. They called these moods "the dark night of the soul." Many saints have even shown neurotic symptoms. So, too, the ordinary penitent, striving hard for sanctity, may find himself in a state in which he feels that God has turned against him. Why God allows this, we don't know. But we do know that we ought to recover our sense of balance as soon as possible, face up to our responsibilities, and regain that inner joy that is indispensable in the spiritual life. In other words, give free play to your Christian sense of humor or your Christian sense of values or whatever else you may label it, and get back to your regular confession.

What I have attempted to do in this chapter is to summarize the art of positive thinking on venial sins. I am not referring to the modern peace-of-mind cult that claims you can cure neuroses and physical ailments, improve your personality, and increase your salary by the simple process of thinking positive thoughts. Instead, I have in mind the positive attitude that the classical spiritual writers insist is so necessary in the spiritual life if you are to make progress against the inroads of the venial sins that eat away the substance of the soul. There are two ways of looking at your Catholic faith. One is negative and static: you accept the fact that you were born a Catholic and that's that. You don't get excited about it. You feel that your religion has no right to make any great demands on you, that it need not involve you very deeply, that it is simply one of the amenities of civilized life, with periodical confession as a necessary formality.

The positive attitude, on the contrary, contemplates spiritual development as work to be done, and done to the best of your ability. This may sound awfully American and activistic, so perhaps I had better say that spiritual development is a work of art. Now any work, unless it is brutal and dehumanizing, gives the worker a keen natural pleasure, a certain sense of satisfaction. Once you become used to a job, you take pleasure in it according to the degree of facility with which you do it. Confession of venial sins is work and it is work that ought to engage your enthusiasm. If you put your heart and soul into it, you will find joy in doing it. For you will find that the Holy Spirit, the spirit of joy, will be your co-worker in this task of achieving self-knowledge and self-discipline.

CHAPTER 4

EXAMINATION OF CONSCIENCE

The penitent knows what sins he has committed, and to what degree he was guilty of deliberate and intentional violations of the moral law. He alone can penetrate into his memory, dredge up the past and hand up the evidence against himself. He alone knows what were his inner desires, intentions, passions, and ambitions. He is the only one who can make his examination of conscience — though admittedly he can often be helped by the priest who hears his confession.

Before beginning your examination of conscience, you will find it a salutary practice to say a prayer for light. The Book of Genesis tells how God in the beginning of the world caused light to shine in the darkness. Your soul is a dark, confused mass of good and bad ambitions, emotions and passions, and you need the illumination that comes from the Holy Spirit if you are to see yourself as you really are. That means that the Divine Teacher who dwells within you will gladly help you to see yourself as God sees you.

To properly examine your conscience, you must first know the moral law. I suppose a great many people who are doing wrong things will be saved through their ignorance. The light shines in their darkness and the darkness does not comprehend it. But that cannot be said of the ordinary Catholic. If he has had a Catholic education, he has at least a minimum knowledge of moral law and knows what is wrong. Once in a while you meet a Catholic who claims that the moral theologians are not up to date on the moral problems of his particular department or field of interest and, as a result, he feels he is uncertain as to whether a certain practice or custom is legitimate. True, there are some tough moral problems in business, labor relations, and atomic warfare for which theologians have not yet agreed on solutions. It takes time for theologians to study all angles of new economic or social situations before they can express their theological opinions. But in the ordinary affairs of everyday life, the average Catholic knows the moral rules and their application. One hardheaded old Yankee shipbuilder, when asked why he became a Catholic, said: "Well, the other religions tell you to be good, but the Catholic religion tells you *how* to be good." Catholic moral teaching is not fuzzy. It is specific and definite.

Knowledge of the moral law, however, is only the starting point for an examination of conscience. The important question is: did I violate the moral law? I may know the Commandments by heart and yet have a great amount of difficulty trying to figure out whether or not I broke a Commandment when I listened to a ribald story, or when I told my neighbor off for his drunken party the night before. Here we come to the question of responsibility and it is perhaps the toughest nut to crack in the whole realm of moral problems. Was I guilty when I did this or that act, and to what degree was I responsible? Was I acting under an uncontrollable impulse? You cannot commit a sin unless you intend to commit it and so the question is: how willful and deliberate was my intention?

I don't wish to go into the old controversy about free will. Many a harmless argument we had in college about free will and predestination, the hardy perennials for debating societies. But I do find it strange that today, when there is more talk than ever before about political liberty and the free world, there is in the free world a general trend away from the concept of freedom in economics, sociology, psychiatry, and other sciences. As someone has said, freedom is everywhere in retreat. The trend is toward "determinism." Man is said to have no free will of his own but is simply a machine that is stimulated into action by biological urges or impulses over which he has no control. You find it even in advertising. There is the notion that subconscious motives impel customers to buy and so the advertiser studies motivation, trying to discover the subconscious motive that will cause people to buy his product; and having found the button, he will push it and — presto — the sales will come in.

Yet here is the Catholic Church, often accused of being the enemy of freedom, carrying the banner for free will. She insists that the ordinary man is free, that he presses the button that starts him into action and that he is responsible for pressing the button. In other words, your examination of conscience is not a puppet show of memory. You are looking back in memory to moments when you pulled the strings to acts for which you were responsible. You were not pushed around by impulses. They undoubtedly had an influence on you, but you had the final say. You were master of your actions. One is reminded of the situation of a swimmer. He is surrounded by water and it is pressing him on all sides, but he freely decides to move this way or that.

There are schools of psychiatric thought that maintain nobody is really responsible for his actions, that your decisions are determined by instinctive drives in the unconscious. If that were so, then you would find yourself going along from day to day thinking you were free when actually you would be the slave of those instincts. They would be the cause of your desires and intentions even though you had no idea that they were entering into your decisions.

This line of thinking has appeared even in Catholic theological circles. One Catholic writer, a few years ago, published a book in which he claimed that the average person is not guilty of mortal sins in the case of sexual acts because his unconscious urges force him to do these acts. That is, he may approve or disapprove of his acts but he cannot prevent himself from doing such acts. The passions are so strong that they make him do the very act he hates. Therefore, according to this writer, a person would be guilty of violating the Sixth Commandment not by committing fornication or masturbation, which he cannot prevent himself from doing, but by approving the acts. So if he merely committed a forbidden sexual act, he could go to Communion afterward without going to confession.

Pope Pius XII quickly condemned this notion that sexual passion destroys free will in the ordinary case. He admitted that certain inner pressures do exert a strong influence on the will but he denied that these urges or impulses rob a man of freedom in every case. The Holy Father was thus simply restating the traditional teaching that the moral life is a struggle against the instincts but that the mere fact of struggle doesn't mean that a good moral life is impossible.

I don't want to give the impression that this whole problem of personal responsibility can be solved very simply. The prevalence of the new theories of responsibility and the advances made in the field of psychiatry have prompted even the American courts to re-examine their test of responsibility for crime. For over a hundred years, the American courts have followed a ruling laid down by a British court in 1843 which stated that a man is responsible for his acts if he knows right from wrong. The legal critics of this "M'Naghten ruling" maintain that this test is out of line with our current knowledge of mental illness, which acquaints us with the fact that a man may know the difference between right and wrong but yet he may be unable so save himself from committing a crime because he is forced to do it by some inner compulsion. Therefore, say these critics, no man should be judged guilty of a crime he couldn't prevent. Our State courts, however, are waiting for the various schools of psychiatric thought to agree on a good definition of mental illness before they will abandon the old test of criminal responsibility. As the New Jersey Supreme Court recently said, psychiatry is not an exact science at the present time, and a test based on mental disease would differ "with the psychiatric winds of the moment."

To return to the court of conscience – you examine your conscience on the premise that you have sufficient free will in ordinary affairs to deserve praise or blame for what you do. Catholic moral theologians will not object to the claim that mentally ill persons might commit crimes they have no deliberate intention to commit. What they do object to is the notion that all normal people are mentally ill and cannot control their actions.

There is nothing new in the idea that most of us are unconsciously motivated by many factors when we do an act. Spiritual writers have been telling us that for centuries. They have warned us that vanity sometimes impels us to do an act we think we are doing out of sheer goodness of heart. Then, too, divine grace inspires us to do good acts even though we are usually unconscious of the fact that grace is working in the soul. As Rev. John C. Ford, S.J., and Rev. Gerald Kelly, S.J. point out[1] Catholic theologians have never doubted the freedom of the will even though grace *draws* the will toward good by means of heavenly love. When we are acted upon by an inspiration of grace, we may be aware after the act that our heart was strangely warmed and attracted to the good but usually we are not conscious of grace while we are doing the act. Like the disciples on the way to Emmaus, we do not recognize Christ while He is speaking to our hearts but we do recollect Him in retrospect. How this influence of grace and the freedom of the will can be reconciled is a mystery. How the influence of heredity and

[1] *Contemporary Moral Theology*, Vol. 1 (Westminster, Md.: 1958), p. 198.

environment can be reconciled with free will is also a mystery. How urges and instincts and free will can be reconciled is another mystery. But as Fathers Ford and Kelly sum it up: "To influence is not to compel."

We welcome the findings of psychiatrists and psychoanalysts. These men, working like the priest to combat human misery, are making rapid advances in the study of mental illness and this is a great blessing, especially in view of the fact that the number of mentally disturbed persons is increasing in the United States at an alarming rate. Moreover, in curing mental ills, the psychiatrists and psychoanalysts are removing obstacles that interfere with the free functioning of the will. You can hardly expect a man to live a good moral life if his mind is tormented by anxieties, conflicts, and disordered impulses. However, while these experts are learning more and more about the subconscious forces that hamper men in making decisions, they have produced thus far no evidence that would warrant the conclusion that subconscious impulses take away free will from the normal person (or as a psychiatrist might say, an emotionally healthy person).

It is true that these subconscious factors can reduce the degree of freedom of will even though they do not take it away entirely. That has always been the teaching of the Church; but we must confess that the tendency among Catholics in the past has been to minimize the part these hidden factors play. We have not made sufficient allowance for the role of these drives in decreasing human responsibility. As Fathers Kelly and Ford say in their book: "The only general rule which we would recommend at present is this: Subjective disabilities and impediments excuse the average man and woman from mortal guilt much more frequently than a reading of moral theology manuals might lead one to suppose."[2]

The practical consequence of all this is that in examining your conscience, it is not enough simply to remember that

[2] *Ibid.*, p. 239.

you did such and such a wrong act. The core of the sin is in the intention, and unless you had a sinful intention, the external act was not a sin. If you ate meat on Friday, forgetting what day it was, you had no intention of committing a sin and you need not mention it in confession. Again, your passion may have diminished the deliberateness of your intention and reduced the degree of your guilt. If you are a father and you saw a hoodlum annoying your daughter in the street, maybe you went after him with a murderous punch. The passion of anger reduced your degree of freedom, and while your act was deliberate, it was not as malicious as it would have been if you were attacking an innocent bystander.

If you think you may have committed a serious sin, try to remember your mental state at the time you committed the act. For the important thing is to prepare in your examination to give the priest the facts and the internal facts are usually more important than the external act. Of course the priest will do his best to help you decide how guilty you were but don't leave all the work to the priest. Your conscience will usually tell you just how responsible you were.

Take into account the conscious influence that you know entered into the act. Maybe you ate meat on Friday because of fear of embarrassing your non-Catholic friends. Tell that to the priest. The unconscious influences will, however, be more elusive. You can't run out to the psychiatrist to get him to help you decide what made you do the act. So roll up your sleeves and recollect your mental state. Don't judge yourself too sternly or too easily. Be honest with yourself. Why did you tell that whopper of a lie? Was it because you are what people call a constitutional liar, or because you trifle with truth, or because you hate the person you lied to and have boasted you wouldn't give him the right time, or because you really liked him and were sparing him from the awful truth, or because you were trying to protect yourself?

These factors did not force you to commit the sin but they do shed light on the degree of malice in your heart at the time you committed the sin.

I am speaking, of course, of examination of conscience at times when you know beyond any doubt you have committed a mortal sin. Here it is important to dig around the roots of the sin to find how deep was your malice. If your confession is a devotional confession, that is, if you are not at all conscious of any serious sin, then of course you need not go through any rigorous study of your mental states.

Since there is no obligation to confess venial sins, all that is really necessary is to tell one venial sin or some sin of your past life which has already been forgiven. Therefore, there is no obligation to make an examination of conscience for venial sins. The Council of Trent seems to address itself to meticulous penitents when it states bluntly: "Venial sins may be concealed in confession without guilt."[3] "From this principle it follows," says Father Scharsch, "that those act foolishly who torment themselves for hours in examining their consciences in order to confess all their faults with the greatest possible completeness."[4]

There are penitents who sweat blood on this futile task of hunting up every last venial sin. It's impossible to reconstruct every moment of the past in order to decide how much deliberateness went into each venial sin, how much negligence, how much pleasure. Usually your mortal sins stand out like sore thumbs in your memory and you need make only a little effort to remember just how you felt at the time of the unhappy episode. But if you are going to be rigorous about your venial sins, you will soon find that there is a spot of guilt in practically all your actions, just as you can hardly breathe without inhaling some particle of dust. Your motives are so confoundedly mixed, even in your good actions, that

[3] Session 14, chap. 5.
[4] Scharsch, *op. cit.*, p. 74.

some evil seems always to be creeping in. But you have to remember that the Christian life is designed to take care of these venial sins.

As I mentioned in the last chapter, there are many ways in which you can have venial sins forgiven besides confession. It's a comforting thought that you are, even though you may not realize it, constantly atoning for sins. The next time you pass up a juicy steak on Friday, remember you are not merely observing a law but perhaps satisfying for your venial sins with your sacrifice. In the Psalms you find reference to "hidden sins." Possibly King David had venial sins in mind especially — the little offenses we forget because they are so slight. Since the whole Christian life is a penance, there is no need to haggle over your venial sins the way you would about your mortal sins. Perhaps the slight trespasses you manage to bring to light after laborious self-scrutiny have already been forgiven by your kindness to your neighbor or by reception of Holy Communion.

I don't think it is possible to overstress the venial sinner's need to look to the future and the purpose of amendment rather than to the sins of the past. If you are a devotional penitent, keep your eyes fixed on spiritual progress. You are not writing a "true confession" for one of those lurid magazines that defile our newsstands. You are not an archaeologist rummaging around in the ruins of a dead past. You are interested in what you hope to become, not what you were. So don't exhaust yourself over peccadilloes in your examination of conscience.

When a business executive tries to discover what has been holding up the flow of orders in his department, he is not interested in the mistakes themselves. He is interested in making progress. Someone has said that the only thing we learn from history is that we never learn from history. This points out a great truth. If you know the mistakes of your past and don't use this knowledge to do better in the future, then it is just a mass of useless information. You examine your conscience, if at all, to help stimulate you to improve in the future. Therefore, unless you suspect you have committed mortal sins, don't try to be mathematically exact in your examination of conscience. Thank God, you are not an IBM machine. Take no more than five minutes at the most for your examination and don't attempt any agonizing reappraisal of your past blunders. Concentrate on a serene, determined resolve to live close to Christ. This will benefit you more than any bookkeeping operation. "O God, my whole soul longs for thee as a deer for running water; my whole soul thirsts for God, the living God" (Ps. 41:6). The very fact that you take the trouble to go to confession is proof of your desire to love God. You may think your desire is a rather bland affair but if you concentrate on it, you will find it is a sharp knife that cuts away the cancer of sin.

Father Scharsch gives two methods for confessing venial sins.[5] These methods, by the same token, are methods for examining conscience on venial sins. The first method is to try to gather up all your energies and focus all your attention on all the venial sins you can possibly remember which you have committed since the last confession. This may be a good practice for saints but I don't think it works for ordinary people. It may develop your memory but I don't think it will develop your spiritual life; and there is a real danger that you will find yourself confessing sins for which you are not sorry. St. Francis de Sales said it is an "abuse" to confess small or great sins if we do not intend to avoid them.

The second method is to concentrate your attention and sorrow on one or two venial sins committed since your last confession. This seems to be a more effective method for the average person. The first method gives you a shotgun coverage of all your sins but the second concentrates your attention on one or two targets. Make a complete tour of inspection

[5] Scharsch, *op. cit.*, pp. 80–86.

of your soul but after you have decided which are the worst venial sins, then attach the full weight of your attention and amendment to them. Mark them down in your memory in big letters.

This subject reminds me of the problem of making New Year's resolutions. If you note all the faults of the past year and resolve to shed them, you probably won't live up to any of your resolutions. But if you make only a few and very definite resolutions, you have a better chance of success. There is an old maxim, "Divide and conquer," but this is one case in which it doesn't work. Don't divide your attention among many venial sins. Concentrate on one or two so you can focus your sorrow on them.

How can you distinguish a mortal sin from a venial sin? This is not an easy question to answer in particular cases, but according to the Council of Trent, it is a matter of faith that there is a distinction between mortal and venial sins. Most heretics have rejected any such distinction, some of them holding that all sins deserve the same punishment, others claiming that all acts of good men are virtuous and all acts of bad men are evil. Luther said that all sins of unbelievers are mortal and all sins of believers, except infidelity, are venial. Scripture does not use the terms *mortal* and *venial* but the idea is certainly there. St. John says that some sins are "unto death" and others are "not unto death," and St. Paul (1 Cor. 3:8–15) describes the distinction between serious and light sins in a passage in which he signifies venial sins by the term *wood, hay and stubble.*

The three requisites of a mortal sin are grievous matter, sufficient reflection, and full consent of the will. First, grievous matter. Unless the offense itself was a serious matter, you did not commit a mortal sin. A girl doesn't break off her engagement simply because her boy friend has committed some slight discourtesy. God does not break off His friendship with us because of a slight offense. Those offenses which directly and grossly dishonor Him are mortal sins, such as hatred of God, idolatry, sacrilegious Communion, blasphemy, perjury. Then there are sins against faith and hope. Finally, serious sins against the neighbor such as murder, physical assaults, calumny, adultery. Some of these sins may become venial through "smallness of matter." But if the sins are directly against God, they do not admit of smallness of matter. Blasphemy in itself is always a serious matter.

The second requisite of a mortal sin is sufficient reflection. As long as you knew at least in a confused way that the act was wrong when you did it, then you had sufficient reflection. Maybe your reflection did not last during the entire time of the wrong act or maybe you did not reflect on the malice of the act. Nevertheless you had sufficient reflection as long as you knew the act was wrong when you did it. If you didn't know it was wrong when you did it but discovered later on that it was a forbidden act, then it was not a mortal sin. You must have known it was wrong at the time of the act or else it was not a mortal sin for you.

Some claim that mortal sins are very, very rare and that in order to commit a mortal sin, a sin that would kill the life of the soul, you would have to be so malicious as in effect to shake your fists at God. It is laudable to hope that few mortal sins are committed and even to say that a genuine mortal sin is rarer than most people think. It is going too far, however, to say that we must believe there is Hell but we don't have to believe there is anyone in it, or to say, as one devout soul did, that we are all saved because the parable tells us that ninety-nine sheep were saved and only one lost and eventually even he was saved.

The Church has no statistics on the number of mortal sins committed but its teaching on mortal sin does imply that they are all too common. Certainly you can commit a mortal sin without shaking your fists at God. Perhaps you do not advert to God at all. As a matter of fact, I think most persons who commit mortal sins never think of God at the time of the sin. Their guilt derives from the fact that they are doing something they know is forbidden.

"Full consent of the will" means simply that you had the choice of doing or not doing the act. It does not mean full approval of the act. Maybe you had grave reservations about the act, maybe you did it with reluctance, with a bad conscience, and perhaps the act was repulsive to a certain degree. As long as you had the ability to brush these factors aside and make a decision, then you had full consent. In practically every sin, there are some repulsive features but you decide to sin because you are attracted to some pleasing feature of the sin. You never choose to do evil for the sake of evil. You choose to do it for something about it that strikes you as good. Suppose I steal a basket of spinach. I hate spinach so I don't steal for the sake of the thing I hate; but I steal it so as to be able to tell my friends about the clever way in which I stole it. The anticipated pleasure of describing my triumph is what appeals to me. I can't imagine a man sinning just for the sin of it, but I can imagine him sinning just for the fun of it.

Notice that I am speaking in the above paragraphs about the normal person. The normal person (i.e., the emotionally healthy person) knows right from wrong and can resist doing wrong and has free will. There are abnormal persons, or normal persons in thoroughly abnormal situations, who know what is wrong but cannot resist doing it. A man under the influence of liquor, for example, may know that certain acts are wrong but he does them nevertheless because his condition has taken away his freedom. His mind may be keen but his will is helpless. Actually he is not responsible for what he does when he is drunk unless he could have reasonably foreseen what he might do. In his beastly stupor he is not capable of doing a human act. He is, of course, responsible for getting drunk but that is something else again. It is conceivable, too, that certain persons addicted to sexual sins may know they are doing wrong but their passions may rob them of free will. These cases, however, are abnormal and my remarks about sufficient reflection and full consent were meant to apply only to normal penitents.

The obligation to make an examination of conscience, when there are mortal sins, is a strict one. For after all, one mortal sin can mean the difference between salvation and damnation. The old maxim rings insistently in our ears: "What doth it profit a man. . . ." Mussolini's adviser during the Lateran pact negotiations, Counsellor Barone, was reconciled to the Church during the bargaining and died before the pact was signed. Pope Pius XI, even though quite disturbed for fear the pact might fall through, said: "The salvation of a single soul is worth infinitely more than a settlement of the Roman Question." As a matter of fact, the duty to examine conscience on mortal sins is so rigorous that a confessor must send away a penitent unabsolved if he judges that he has failed to make a good examination.

The obligation is, of course, less severe for the sick. That is why a hospital chaplain will brush off the excuse of a patient who says he needs more time to make his examination. This excuse might be just a dodge to put off confession to a later date and the experienced priest will soon recognize it as a delaying tactic. He will explain to the sick person that a thorough examination is not necessary for him, and if the priest has the time and cares to do so, he may ask the patient questions with the intention of uncovering serious sins. Frequently this is impossible as the patient is too weak for a sustained inquiry, or perhaps the doctor is waiting impatiently outside the door, or the priest himself has too many other calls to permit him to spend a long time with one patient.

Formal examinations of conscience are printed in prayer books or catechisms. Some persons find them helpful; others are only confused by the profusion and complexity of the questions. A common and quite successful method is to run through the Commandments of God, the Commandments of the Church, and the duties of your state of life. The chief difficulty for many penitents lies in answering the question about fulfilling the duties of your state in life. Time marches on and the revolutionary changes in modern life make it hard for us to know just what our state of life prescribes for us in the way of personal responsibilities. Suppose you are a television executive. It's not easy to decide just what degree of responsibility you have toward your audience, not only in the matter of obscenity and violence but also with regard to the general quality level of the material presented. Just what your responsibility is in the matter of raising standards is something you will have to struggle with. Yes, you have general moral principles to guide you but the application of these is a monumental task that requires absolute honesty, prudence, and common sense. So it is in many other fields where a man has a position of influence. He is using his God-given talents among the children of God and so his responsibility to God is most serious, especially where he is involved with great masses of people.

There is one helpful source of remembered sins that most of us never tap in our examination of conscience. It is the comments of the neighbors. Some of us feel it's bad enough to have to live with the Joneses without having to listen to them. Our complacent ears might as well be stuffed with cotton for all the attention we give to neighbors' comments. I know we should not nurse a craving for "human respect" but at the same time a good reputation is a precious thing and we ought to deserve it. Let gossips buzz and character assassins fling their dirt, but are we sure that all the neighbors are always wrong in what they say about *us*? As Father Scharsch says: "Hatred has keen eyes."

In a religious community, the honest but outspoken comments of the brethren serve to polish off many a rough corner of a man's character. At least some of your neighbors are capable of fair and honest comment. What do they say about you? Think it over in your next examination of conscience. We are too ready to assure ourselves the neighbor is just a no-good windbag and we stop our ears so that we hear no evil. A certain writer of American history went to live in Europe in order to get a better perspective on his own country. Likewise your next-door neighbor is liable to have a better perspective on your character and habits than you have. If you sincerely try to be objective in your examination, your neighbor's comments and the Holy Spirit can break the spell of your self-enchantment.

Scrupulous persons are advised not to make a thorough examination. The more they scrutinize themselves, the more tense they become. For them it is enough that they have a general desire to confess and amend. They should be forbidden, moreover, to think about their examination once they have left the confessional, else they will blame themselves day after day for having made a faulty examination. (The study of the special problems of the scrupulous I have left for Chapter 10.)

If you are not plagued by scruples and suspect that you have committed mortal sins since your last confession, then the need of an examination of conscience is imperative. You are preparing to present your case to the confessor and you should prepare it so that he will have all the evidence necessary for him to make a decision. He must forgive all or nothing. Half a moon may be better than no moon at all, as the old song had it, but half a confession is not better than no confession. As a matter of fact, half a confession is a lot worse than no confession because it is a sacrilege. The priest cannot reconcile you to God as long as one mortal sin still remains; for just as he cannot baptize you as a half-Catholic, so he cannot render you a half-friend of God. He cannot force God to coexist with sin in the soul, for mortal sin of its very nature drives God out of the soul. In other words, if you conceal one mortal sin, then you make it impossible for the priest to absolve you.

I refer of course to a deliberate concealment of a mortal sin. If you make a serious examination and yet somehow forget a mortal sin, you can be absolved. When you honestly intend to tell all your sins your sorrow covers even the sin you forget. But this is quite a different case from that of a man who maliciously hides a serious sin. He may fool the priest into saying the words of absolution, but he does not fool God, and God will not send down His forgiveness through the priest.

The Council of Trent condemns those who say that it is not necessary to confess all mortal sins of which a man is conscious after a diligent search.[6] I mention this since there is reason to believe that certain penitents today do withhold the sin of birth control from the priest. They apparently rationalize it on the ground that it's no concern of the priest, but the penitent's own private affair. How many such penitents there are is a big question but we do know that the use of contraceptives is a prevalent practice in the United States, and secular attitudes do affect at least those Catholics who are weak in the faith. Pollsters from time to time quiz people on their views on birth control and the published statistics say that a high percentage of Catholics practice birth control. It's true that figures lie and liars figure, but I feel quite sure that many Catholics do practice birth control today just as Catholics in past eras adopted sinful practices that were popular at the time, such as dueling. How many Catholics use contraceptives is not an issue. As someone said, morality is not a matter of mathematics, i.e., an immoral practice is evil whether one person or a hundred million regard it as legitimate. Majority vote is a sensible way of deciding who will get a political office but it's rather absurd

[6] Session XIV, can. 7.

to take a vote on the immutable law of God. It's almost like voting for or against the Atlantic Ocean.

From time to time magazine articles appear in which the authors dexterously assume that the wise, old Catholic Church will ultimately change its stand on birth control. Probably some Catholics who conceal the sin in confession operate on the premise that they are hiding a harmless practice which the Church will eventually approve, and therefore they are not really hiding a sin. What their subjective guilt is in the eyes of God, we don't know; but we do wish they would either stay away from confession altogether or else make a complete confession. If they think that certain psychological or social or financial pressures diminish their guilt, they should mention this to the confessor rather than conceal the sin altogether. The priest knows that marital chastity is exceedingly difficult, especially in slum districts of our big cities.

You may have noticed that the Council of Trent said that you must confess all sins of which you are conscious "after a diligent search." The diligence required is the degree of diligence that you generally give to any matter you consider important. The examination, therefore, need not be a hair-raising experience. As long as you have used ordinary care in making your search, then you need not worry. If, after making your confession following diligent search, you find you have forgotten to tell a mortal sin, don't get upset about it. Simply confess it at a later time.

You may have a poor memory. That's a fault of the physical organism, not of your intention. If a violin is broken, you may have the best intentions in the world and still you cannot get music out of it. If the physical organism allied to memory fails to work, that is not your fault. God is interested in effort rather than actual performance, more in intention than in results. For we can control our intentions but often we have no control of the forces that produce results. Remember that the important point in the examination is an *if: if* you remember a mortal sin, then you must tell it. Possibly you feel ashamed of it but that is no excuse. As the Council of Trent says: "If the sick man is ashamed to show his wounds to the physician, the latter cannot cure what is unknown to him."[7]

At missions and retreats you have been told that you must confess the number, kind, and circumstances of your sins. This sounds like a tall order. The fact, is however, that you will do this automatically if you are using ordinary diligence in your examination. The small boy who was impressed by the word *prose* was surprised when told he had been speaking prose all his life without realizing it. So you have undoubtedly been confessing your sins according to number, kind, and circumstances without thinking of them in those precise terms.

What do the terms mean? If you have missed Mass a number of times, you don't merely say "I missed Mass." You make at least a rough guess about the number of times you missed. Perhaps it will be: "I have missed Mass about four times." If the mortal sin is a habit with you, tell how long the habit has lasted since your last confession. You need not torture your memory trying to compute mathematically how many times you committed the sin each day. Probably it would be a futile task. This is specially important in the case of those who have a habit of willfully entertaining impure or angry thoughts. The priest is not a Univac and he will not be impressed by astronomical numbers. Just tell how long the habit has been bothering you since your last confession.

As to the kind of sins, you ought to specify. Obviously you wouldn't be giving the priest much of a clue if you simply said: "I have sinned in thought." Examine yourself to see whether the thought was one of anger or impurity or

[7] Session XIV, chap. 5.

jealousy. No need to give him the colorful details of sexual sins. Some penitents imagine they are hiding something if they withhold picturesque details, but the confessional is not a divorce court, so you need not tell the seamy side of your sins. In fact, the moral theologians advise confessors against asking questions about details of sexual sins. On the other hand, it is not enough merely to say, "I have broken the sixth Commandment." You should tell whether it was a sin of self-abuse, adultery, or an impure thought. In the case of the seventh Commandment, it makes a big difference whether the sin was robbery, embezzlement, extortion, or filching a dime from a piggy bank.

It is necessary also to confess the circumstances under which the mortal sins were committed; that is, provided the circumstances are relevant. It doesn't make any difference whether the victim of your knockout punch was a Democrat or a Republican, or whether you had a bad thought on top of the Empire State building or on the deck of the Staten Island ferry. Those circumstances don't make the sin any less or greater. But it does make a difference whether you swear in the Yankee Stadium or in your parish church on Sunday morning at Solemn Mass.

Sometimes circumstances radically change the entire character of a sin. A single man commits a serious sin when he has sexual relations with a woman, but the sin is doubly grave if the woman is married and he knows it. Sometimes the circumstances may not actually change the character of the sin but may increase its guilt. It is far more culpable to unjustly strike a child than an adult. However, it is hard for the ordinary penitent to decide in each case just what does and does not change the character of the sin, so it is enough for him to give the priest some brief description of the sin. The exception is a sexual sin. Try to remember sexual sins in broad outline without bothering about details. In short, use your discretion in telling circumstances of sins.

In attempting to decide whether certain factors change a sin from venial to mortal, it is well to keep in mind these points: (1) If the penitent intended to commit a mortal sin, he committed a mortal sin. (2) If he did something that he knew was a venial sin but also knew someone else would be led into mortal sin as a result of it, then he committed a mortal sin. (3) If he teased a person he knew would become violently angry, he committed a mortal sin. (4) If he did something that was slight in itself but by so doing willfully put himself into an occasion of serious sin, then he committed a mortal sin.

On the other hand, what has all the appearances of a mortal sin may be no sin at all or may be only venial. If the penitent ate less than two ounces of meat on Friday, his sin was venial. If he ate meat on Friday, unaware it was Friday, or missed Mass on Sunday, not knowing it was Sunday, he committed no sin. If there was lack of full consent, there was only a slight sin or none at all. For instance, he may have had an impure thought while half-asleep. If he committed some serious violation of the Commandments but didn't realize it was serious, it could not have been mortal. Some sins are so prevalent in certain localities that children begin to think they are only slightly immoral. Vandalism is so rife in certain sections of New York City that I feel sure that some hoodlums don't realize the seriousness of their offenses.

How about sins that are doubtful? First, you may be in doubt as to whether you ever really committed a certain act, e.g., eating meat on Friday. Where you have no positive reason for thinking you have committed an act, then you need not confess it. Or, if you have no positive reason for thinking a certain act was a mortal sin, e.g., attending a certain movie, you don't have to confess this doubtful sin. Let me give you an example. Suppose an acquaintance claims you revealed to him some scandalous information about a certain physician. You can't remember ever having done it, but your acquaintance is generally trustworthy. Another reliable person, however, says you did not reveal the information and that the first person got it from someone else. Here you have a good reason for thinking you committed a mortal sin and another good reason for thinking you did not. The two cancel each other out and you have no obligation to tell the sin in confession.

However, it is recommended that penitents confess even the sins of which they are doubtful for the sake of peace of mind. If you do, be sure to confess them as doubtful, which means that if you have no other sins since your last confession besides these doubtful sins, then you will have to confess some sin of your past life. For doubtful sins are not material for absolution. What I have said about doubtful sins does not apply to the scrupulous. They should shun telling doubtful sins as they would the plague. Conversely, the lax ought to be urged to tell doubtful sins. If you are generally lax, the presumption is that what you consider doubtful was actually a mortal sin.

What about a person who has confessed a sin as doubtful and then later remembers that it was definitely a mortal sin? Must he confess it? The most common opinion among theologians is that he need not confess it again.

But suppose a man has committed a serious sin and doubts whether or not he confessed it? If he has some good reason to think he confessed it, then he need not tell it again. A man who is accustomed to making a good examination may presume he did so on this occasion as well. Scrupulous people, however, should be forbidden to reconfess unless they have some extraordinary reason for doing so. The general rule, then, is that the normal person need not reconfess but may do so if it will give him peace of mind.

Converts who are baptized unconditionally at the time of their reception into the Church, having never before been baptized in any sect, are under no obligation to confess sins committed before baptism. The sacrament wipes away all sin. They are figuratively buried in the water as Christ was buried in the tomb and they rise up to a new glorified life as Christ rose on Easter. Usually the convert has such unquestioning faith in the sacrament of baptism and such a healthy attitude toward sin, that he is only too glad to be excused from making his confession.

But suppose the convert has already been baptized in a Protestant sect. This raises a difficulty. The original baptism may or may not have been valid. It's possible that the baptism was performed in the wrong way. For example, I know of one church in which the minister poured the water while the choir sang the words. Or it is possible that the minister at the time of baptism did not have an intention to give new life to the soul but simply looked on baptism as a formal initiation ceremony into his church, a ceremony that produced no interior effect at all. In most of these Protestant baptisms, only God knows whether they were valid or not. Some of them are just as valid as baptisms by Catholic priests, some are not. So the only thing for a priest to do, since the original baptism of the convert was doubtfully valid, is to baptize him conditionally: "If you are not baptized, I baptize you in the name of the Father, and of the Son, and of the Holy Spirit." Then the priest will hear his confession of the sins of his whole life.

If his first baptism was valid, that original rite wiped away all sins he committed up to the time of that first baptism but he has been committing sins between the time of his first baptism and the Catholic ceremony, and these need to be forgiven and are forgiven by the priest in confession. If, on the other hand, his first baptism was invalid for some reason or other, then he has sins on his soul since he was a child and all these are wiped away by the valid baptism by the priest. This means that the absolution given by the priest in confession after the baptism had no effect because, fortunately, there were no sins left to pardon, all having been forgiven by baptism.

How long should we take in making our examinations? There is no rule of thumb except that for devotional confessions, five minutes is generally long enough. With mortal sins, you need whatever time is necessary for a diligent search. This will depend largely on the length of time you have been away from confession. You don't have to make a dramatic production out of it like a woman shopper examining a dress. The Church asks only for reasonable diligence.

Ordinarily there is a strict obligation to tell all your mortal sins. Maybe it will be humiliating to tell certain sins or maybe you know the priest will lose his good impression of you or maybe there is a long line waiting outside the confessional. Nevertheless, the obligation to confess binds despite these factors. But there are some conditions that do allow for an incomplete confession. Obviously moral impossibility is one. A person who is very sick is morally incapable of making a complete confession. This is specially true in a battle or in an accident when the priest cannot get around to each injured person to hear all his sins. Then the priest can give absolution to the group. The noted Father Maturin was last seen on the bridge of the Lusitania giving absolution to the passengers about to be engulfed by the swirling waters.

If the priest himself is dying, he may grant absolution before hearing a full confession. This only applies if there is no other priest around. In all these cases, the priest makes sure that the penitents have contrition — in so far as he can be sure. Even in a disaster at sea the priest may ask the victims to make an act of contrition and show some sign of sorrow. He will tell them that if they survive, they should be sure to make another confession, this time in detail.

What about confessing a sin that may seriously harm the reputation of another person who is known to the confessor?

Theologians recommend that the penitent go to a confessor who does not know the person involved. However, the penitent is not bound to take time out and spend money to search for another confessor; for he is not obliged to confess a sin, no matter how serious, if he would thereby injure another person's good name. In fact, he should withhold the sin. The reason for this is that the duty to respect another's good reputation takes precedence over the duty to make a complete confession. In practice it is best not to mention any names at all in confession whether you praise or blame the persons concerned.

CHAPTER 5

CONFESSION

Having examined your conscience, roused your contrition and resolved to amend, you are ready to step into the confessional. You take your place in the queue of waiting penitents. This waiting line forms according to a different pattern in different churches. The custom in some churches is for the penitents to sit in line in a pew near the confessional, gliding along the pew as the person at the head of the line leaves to enter the confessional. The more common practice in the United States, however, is for the penitents to stand in line at either side of the confessional. When you stand in line, try to keep a respectable distance between yourself and the confessional so that you can't hear what is being said inside. It is embarrassing for all concerned if the priest has to leave the confessional to urge penitents to move away a few feet.

It would be wrong, of course, to eavesdrop outside the confessional, but my guess would be that deliberate eavesdropping seldom occurs. As a matter of fact, the average penitent feels mighty uncomfortable if he unintentionally overhears a part of another's confession. However, you can rest assured you have done nothing wrong if you accidentally hear something another penitent or the confessor has said. Occasionally a penitent talks so loud that you can't help hearing him. This would become culpable only if you relayed the information to others. Waiting in a confessional line must have been quite a breath-taking experience when the

Curé of Ars was hearing confessions. Sometimes he would leave the confessional, tap a penitent on the shoulder and tell him that the penitent was needed at home immediately.

Catholic magazines sometimes run stories dealing with the bad manners of penitents on the waiting line. I remember especially a Catholic picture periodical that featured a humorous commentary on confession-line abuses that I thought was very effective. But there has been, I believe, a steady improvement in penitents' manners over the past thirty years. Possibly the prevalence of Catholic education is responsible for the improvement or perhaps people today have more leisure time on Saturday afternoon than formerly and are therefore less impatient. Most penitents now seem to agree with Longfellow that all things come round to him who waits. You don't find the pious halfback who used to make an end run around the line to dash into the confessional ahead of everyone else. Nor do you meet the chatterbox who used to yak-yak in line as if she were waiting for a movie. Or am I imagining things like the old farmer who thought his geese were becoming swans?

These days the penitent who fails to observe the formalities on the waiting line is not deliberately rude. Usually the trouble is that he is an outsider who is unfamiliar with the local customs in this particular church. Maybe he will dash into the confessional out of turn simply because he doesn't realize that in this church the penitents are waiting in a pew instead of alongside the confessional. The important thing is to find out what are the confessional customs in any church where you are intending to make your confession. And remember that if you travel in other countries, you will often find confessional customs that are radically different from those of American churches. Don't be surprised to see male penitents in Europe kneeling directly at the feet of the confessor who has his hand on the penitent's shoulder like a good father welcoming the prodigal son.

I should like to make two general suggestions pertaining to the waiting period. First, keep your mind strictly on your confession. The family may be waiting for you to cook the dinner, but first things first: your confession. The policeman may be sticking a ticket on your car, but keep your mind on your infractions of the divine law. Second, and this is a regrettable but very necessary caution: don't leave your purse in the pews. Thieves are fond of churches where the pickings are lush on Saturday afternoons.

Your confession begins with a formula. I believe the most commonly used formula is: "Bless me, Father, for I have sinned. It is .... weeks since my last confession." So, when the confessor opens the slide and says, "God bless you," you respond with the above words or whatever salutation you prefer. Some penitents like to begin with the Confiteor, which used to be the standard practice. Today, because it takes so long and holds up the waiting line, it is better to say the Confiteor outside the confessional before entering.

After the formal beginning, confess whatever sins you have discovered in your examination of conscience. Shakespeare said that a soft, gentle, and low voice is an excellent thing in a woman. It is excellent in both a man and a woman in the confessional. Speak distinctly as well as audibly. The confessional is not a class in diction, so the confessor does not demand the properly clipped consonant and the orotund vowel, but he does expect you to make a reasonable effort to speak clearly.

Tell the truth, the whole truth, and nothing but the truth. (I am speaking, of course, of mortal sins, not of venial sins. As I mentioned in an earlier chapter, you are not bound to confess venial sins.) It is hard to imagine anyone deliberately lying to Christ in the confessional and I would judge such duplicity to be comparatively rare. The great majority of penitents detest sin and want to make a clean breast of it. However, there are some persons who are deathly afraid of what the priest might think or say and they throw a fog of obscurity around their sins by talking fast and furiously. Others decide they will pare down their confession to what they consider the bare essentials lest the priest should imagine they are worse than they actually are. The result is that they tell their sins in carefully studied phrases, thus skipping over some of the essentials and giving the impression that their sins are trifles. One penitent may confess cryptically that she was unkind to a neighbor, neglecting to mention she calumniated her neighbor and that it was a scalding, bitter jealousy that caused the remark. Another penitent may confess he was overaffectionate with a girl friend, omitting the fact that the girl friend was married, that their meeting was deliberately planned, and that he was quite aware from previous escapades that being alone with her was an occasion of sin for him.

In some cases the priest may be deceived by these little games of hide-and-seek but usually after long years of hearing confessions, he has developed a spiritual radar for detecting subterfuge. He will probably look on these dodges as rather pathetic maneuvers by which the penitent is defeating his own purpose in coming to confession, i.e., to give himself to God. Yet the confessor knows that the good God has a sense of humor and infinite compassion, so he will patiently set about asking the penitent questions that will bring out the full truth.

The real root of the trouble in these cases is not deliberate mendacity but too little awareness of Christ's sacramental presence and too sensitive an awareness of the priest's presence. What is needed, I think, is not a jolt from the confessor but a keener realization on the part of the penitent that the priest is God's priest. The priest in confession, as at the altar, is God's ambassador doing God's work for God's people and trying to be another Christ to sinners. If you are in trouble in a foreign country, you will seek out the American consul, knowing he will do what he can for you precisely because you are an American. God's representative in the confessional will do all he can for you; but think of him not as a private person but as God's envoy ready to help you out of a bad situation. Don't beat around the bush by using weasel words. Be open and honest with him and don't worry about the impression you make on him as a person. You don't go to confession to impress the priest, any more than you receive Communion to impress the celebrant of the Mass. Confession is a "conversion," a turning away from creatures, but a turning toward God. You are not turning toward the priest.

In speaking of those timorous souls who scrimp on details and abbreviate their confession too much, I didn't mean to cast any reflection on penitents who strive for genuine brevity. Be "short and sweet" for brevity is a sign of a good confession as it is also the soul of wit. Make your long story as brief as you possibly can without omitting anything essential. Don't tell what a "devil" your husband is in rousing you to anger. Don't give a colorful biography of your mother-in-law. Some penitents mention irrelevant facts probably to win the confessor's sympathy or even his praise. They describe how tearfully remorseful they felt right after the sin, or what college they attended, or how many novenas they make — all of which are quite irrelevant to this confession.

Father Alban Butler,[1] in stating that confession should be humble as well as brief, added a quaint remark about modesty in dress. (We must remember that he wrote more than a century ago.) He said that the confession should be made "according to custom, on the knees, uncovered, and having put off spurs and swords." In this democratic age of the common man, there's not much danger that men will enter the confessional wearing hats, spurs, and swords, although occasionally you will find a woman in a riding habit or

[1] Rev. Alban Butler, *Meditations and Discourses* (Dublin: James Duffy, 1840), p. 285.

slacks waiting in the confessional line. Much better for them to come to confession thus arrayed rather than not to come at all. There used to be a notion that women should not enter the confessional wearing gloves. Where the notion arose I don't know but I suppose it came from the old days when knighthood was in flower and the noble dame showed her humility by removing the outward signs of her rank.

After you have recited your sins, the priest may ask you questions. If he thinks you have made a complete confession, he will probably make no inquiries at all. If, however, he thinks you have not told all, or if he suspects that your confession is incomplete in some way, he will ask questions. In fact, he is bound to do so else he would not be performing his duty as judge. If he has any idea that you are holding back some fact out of ignorance or shame or forgetfulness, he will put questions to you about the number or circumstances of your sins. Then, too, he may want to find out what is your disposition of soul in order to offer you advice and impose a penance that would be helpful to you in your particular situation. So don't resent the priest's questions. He is simply trying to do his duty as minister of the sacrament. The Church has solemnly warned him that he must not become a mere absolution machine into which you put a confession and out comes an absolution. Besides, he knows more of the doctrine pertaining to confession than does the ordinary penitent and he can be of immense help with his questions.

Lancelot Sheppard, in his *Portrait of a Parish Priest,*[2] tells how the Curé of Ars used to recall long-forgotten sins to his penitents. Others, away a long time, were reminded of the exact time of their last confession. However, you can be quite sure you won't meet with priests who have such extraordinary psychic powers.

At the same time you will find the priest not unreasonable

[2] Newman: Westminster, Md., 1958, p. 158.

in his questions. He is not bound to find out anything over and above what the penitent is bound to confess. He won't ask inappropriate or irrelevant questions. He won't ask the street sweeper if he has embezzled trust funds, or the father of a family if he has practiced poverty. Perhaps he may ask you if you have "anything else" on your conscience. He is not prying or even implying that you have other sins. He is simply trying to help you. Even if the priest thinks that by prodding you he may be able to turn up some new sins, he will probably not trouble you, as he has been warned not to make confession odious to the penitent by grilling him in heavy-handed fashion.

This is especially true in regard to sins of impurity. The priest will be discreet in this department lest he give the impression of having a morbid curiosity or lest he cause teenagers to become inquisitive about sins of which they are ignorant. In fact, if the penitent wants to describe his sexual sins in graphic detail, the priest will tell him that he is quite aware of the general proportions of the offenses and that there is no need to draw pictures. Again, the language used in the confessional ought to be simple and terse, free of foggy circumlocutions. Instead of going all around the mulberry bush, come to the point just as quickly as possible. That doesn't mean you should use the language of the street; not that you would shock the priest, who has probably heard everything in the sin catalogue, but it must be remembered that Christ is present in the sacrament of penance and there is, therefore, never any excuse for vulgarity in the confessional.

If you have been away from confession a long time, the priest will probably ask why. Long absence may indicate a lax conscience and he will be better able to help you if he knows the state of your soul. I find that one question priests have to ask over and over again is: how many times? Be sure to tell him how many times you committed mortal sins so he won't have to ask. If the sin committed is theft, the priest must ask about the amount stolen and if the penitent has made or is willing to make restitution of what he has stolen. He cannot grant absolution unless he exacts this promise of restitution.

As I have already mentioned, if you have not committed any sins since your last confession, you can tell some sin of your past life that has already been forgiven in a past confession. This may seem like carrying coals to Newcastle. If the sins have already been forgiven, it may appear to you superfluous to confess them again. And if you have no sins since your last confession, maybe you think it makes more sense to confess some imperfection such as omitting grace at meals rather than harking back to dead sins of the past? Why does not the Church allow the priest to grant absolution even if there are no sins? What would be the harm in that?

Well, in the first place, it wouldn't make sense. If you approach a friend and assure him you are forgiving him even if he has not offended you, he will think you slightly daffy. Moreover, the Church is sensitively aware of the presence of Christ in confession. The Church doesn't regard confession as a mere ceremony. Absolution is far more than a mumbled formula and a quick sign of the cross. In absolving, the priest sets in motion the sacramental forces. He taps, as it were, the supernatural forces that surround us and calls down the divine mercy. If he sets these forces in motion and they produce no effect, his action is futile and the sacrament is frustrated. To use the theological term, he has subjected the sacrament to the danger of nullity. We protest against a false alarm for a fire, and we have laws to punish those who turn in false alarms. In somewhat the same way, the Church wants to guard against false alarms in the sacramental order.

Now to get back to the main question: why can't we confess mere imperfections if we have no sins to confess since our last confession? Simply because imperfections are not sins and cannot be absolved by the sacrament Christ instituted for the purpose of forgiving sin. Then how about past sins already forgiven? How can the priest forgive again a sin already forgiven? It is the unanimous teaching of theologians that in the case of forgiven sins, the absolution can attach to the renewed sorrow for old sin.

Before a priest absolves you, he must be morally certain you are sorry. The very fact that you are in the confessional is generally proof positive that you are sorry. If you were not sorry, you would not go to the trouble of taking time out to make your confession. But there are cases in which the priest may begin to suspect that the penitent before him is not repentant. Suppose, for instance, that you confess a whopper of a mortal sin in a cool, casual, matter-of-fact tone. Maybe you are actually sorry but trying hard to suppress how much the sin is worrying you. At any rate, the priest has to feel morally certain you are sorry before he can absolve you and if he is uncertain, he will query you about your sorrow.

This situation arises most often when the penitent makes his confession in connection with some external event. For instance, suppose he is to be married the next day and has been told to make his confession so he will be able to receive Communion at the marriage Mass. Or he may belong to an organization that is holding its annual Communion breakfast and he does not want to make himself conspicuous by his absence from the Communion rail. In these cases, the penitent's presence in the confessional will be presumed by the priest to be evidence of his sorrow but the priest is not quite as sure of the penitent's sorrow as he would be in an ordinary confession on a Saturday afternoon. He will listen carefully for anything the penitent might say that would betray a lack of sorrow. If the penitent refuses to remove himself from an immediate occasion of sin, if he balks at forgiving someone who has injured him, if he refuses to make restitution of stolen goods or to stop giving scandal, then the priest will logically conclude he has no real sorrow or desire to amend. If he makes elaborate excuses, or alleges all manner of extenuating circumstances, he will suspect his sincerity. Says St. Augustine: "If thou accuseth thyself, God excuseth thee: if thou excusest thyself, God accuseth thee."

If the priest asks about your sorrow, therefore, he is simply trying to help you. If you are making out an application for a driving license at the State vehicle bureau, you would be only too glad to accept the help of a bureau clerk to fill out the application blank. Likewise the priest is trying to help you meet the requisites for a good confession so that you will receive absolution. He is not trying to make things difficult but he is anxious for you to receive pardon. Suppose your job is for you a proximate occasion of sin. Maybe you feel that you have a good and sufficient reason to remain in this occasion but your confessor may have the impression that you are staying in it for no reason at all and that you could just as easily get a job elsewhere. When he asks you questions, be assured he is hoping to hear a satisfactory answer, for he does want to give you absolution. The very fact that he is asking questions shows that he is trying to save you from making a bad confession. To refuse you absolution is the last thing in the world he wants to do.

One of the duties of the confessor is to instruct the penitent in the essential teachings of the Church or in the duties of his state of life whenever this proves necessary. The priest need not give any instruction to ordinary penitents but there are times when he encounters almost monumental ignorance of the faith. Suppose, for instance, that he is called to the bedside of a man who was baptized but never brought up as a Catholic. Such cases are becoming common today. Divorce has wrecked so many families that some Catholic children never learn the catechism. Then, too, there are unusual cases such as those of soldiers who were baptized in battle areas after a few instructions during the war. Before absolving such persons, the priest would have to be sure they believed in God's existence, that He is a rewarder of good and evil, and in the Trinity, Incarnation, and Redemption. A Catholic nurse can be of invaluable help to the hospital chaplain in preparing the ignorant Catholic for confession.

The more common case, however, is that of a penitent who does not know the duties of his state in life. The priest will instruct him. Maybe he is engaging in some practice which he considers to be a sin but which is no sin at all; or he may be committing some sin, thinking it is worse than it actually is. Some married people have many wrong notions about what is right and what is wrong. Some employees see no sin in failing to put in a day's work; some employers see no sin in exploiting Negro, Mexican, or Puerto Rican laborers.

The priest has a special duty to instruct those who are in a habit of sin. Young boys often develop habits of self-abuse not knowing it is sinful and yet suspecting something is wrong. The priest should prescribe ways and means of preventing relapse into the sin.

The priest will treat an habitual sin in a manner quite different from the clinical manner of the psychiatrist. For the priest must expose to the penitent the shamefulness of the sin in the eyes of God. The psychiatrist, on the other hand, may show his patient that misconduct leads to a hell on earth in the form of neurosis or psychosis. O. Herbert Mowrer, research professor of psychology at the University of Illinois, made this point at a meeting of the American Psychological Association in September, 1959. He did not say sin and mental suffering always go hand in hand but he did say there is a presumption that sin dooms a person to suffering "when it is acutely felt but not acknowledged and corrected."

In confession, the priest's aim is to show that sin leads

to the hell of eternal separation from God. Whereas the psychiatrist gives his patient insight on how his misconduct is leading to personality disorder, the priest wants to show the penitent the shamefulness of sin in the eyes of God. Such a lesson is particularly necessary for those who seldom go to confession and who take sermons against sin "with a grain of salt."

Without derogating from the value of the pulpit, it is a fact that a great many listeners in the pews shrug off sermons. They feel that the preacher is generalizing and so they see no urgent need to apply his strictures on sin to themselves. But in confession the penitent has no doubt as to the identity of the person the priest is talking about. In fact, veteran parish missionaries say that the only successful sermon is the one that brings the sinner to the confessional. They also assert that a missionary does his best work in the confessional and that the missionary ideal is the priest who is a lion in the pulpit and a lamb in the confessional where he can deal firmly with sins and yet with all the sympathetic understanding that Christ, the Lamb of God, showed to the penitent Mary Magdalen.

If you are an habitual sinner, then you can expect to hear the confessor warning you of your danger and exhorting you to take certain measures to prevent relapse into the habit. His is the role of the spiritual physician. Maybe he will recommend regular meditation, prayer, periods of spiritual reading, visits to the Blessed Sacrament. Perhaps he will suggest that you form the habit of making quick aspirations during the day, fiery darts to the heart of God. They are immensely helpful to bring you suddenly to an awareness of His presence. Practice the art of communing with God. What could be a more effective conditioning against temptations than to have a conscious awareness of His presence within you? Perhaps the confessor will suggest a daily examination of conscience or a daily renewal of your resolution to amend. One of the best means of breaking yourself of a bad habit is frequent confession, and the prudent confessor will prescribe it according to your need.

Frequent Holy Communion is also an effective antidote to the poison of sin. It is medicine as well as spiritual food. ". . . behold Him Who takes away the sins of the world," says the priest before distributing Communion at Mass. Holy Communion strengthens the soul against the onslaughts of temptation.

There are other suggestions the priest as physician might prescribe for your habit of sin. He may tell you to stay away from this or that person or place. He may recommend that you set yourself a penalty for falling into sin so that the thought of the penalty itself might help to dissuade you. The priest is anxious to help. Accept his advice. You may have some good reason for thinking his suggestion wouldn't work in your case, but make sure you have a good reason. For after all the priest has had years of experience in handling cases such as yours. He can be an impartial judge, whereas your passions have a vested interest in the sinful habit.

CHAPTER 6

CONTRITION

The Council of Trent states that contrition is a hearty sorrow and detestation of sin coupled with a firm resolve not to sin again. There are three distinct elements in this definition: sorrow, detestation of sin, and the firm resolve not to sin again. The firm resolve is such a broad subject that I will leave it for special treatment in the next chapter. In this present chapter I will discuss sorrow and detestation of sin as separate and distinct factors in contrition. However, it is well to remember that these two elements are always together in this life. They combine to make contrition. Whenever you grieve over sin, you also hate sin, and, conversely, you hate sin whenever you grieve over it.

There are two types of sorrow for sin: perfect and imperfect. Needless to say, perfect sorrow is better than imperfect, but can we imperfect Christians actually experience perfect sorrow? Some think it is easy to come by. After a mission or retreat you will hear parishioners talking quite confidently about gaining plenary indulgences, which means they are quite sure they have that degree of perfect sorrow which is necessary to gain the indulgences. On the other hand, some Catholics have the notion that it's practically impossible for an ordinary mortal to gain a plenary indulgence for the simple reason that the average human being just cannot experience the requisite sorrow.

What is perfect sorrow? It is generally defined as sorrow

that arises from a perfect love of God. This is true, but in addition to having its origin in perfect love of God, perfect sorrow adds something to that love. It is perfect love in sorrow. St. Francis de Sales speaks of a certain type of ruby which assumes a dazzling luster when dropped in vinegar and he points out that perfect love likewise takes on a special luster when impregnated with "the salutary bitterness" of sorrow.

Some psychiatrists speak disparagingly of a sense of guilt and deny it possesses any "salutary" bitterness. They claim it is mentally disturbing and induces unreasonable fears and anxiety. It is true that there can be an unhealthy feeling of guilt that broods over the past in futile worry. Such sick minds need psychiatric care in many cases. But I am here dealing not with the emotion of guilt, but with that conscious, rational sorrow that comes from our realizing that we have cut ourselves off from God. This sense of guilt is healthy, responsible, and reasonable. It is altogether different from the guilt experienced by the ultrasensitive conscience of an emotionally disturbed person who may reveal his inner state by compulsive habits, such as a constant washing of hands.

To think straight on contrition, you have to think of it primarily as an act of the will, not a surge of emotion. In popular songs and words you find "romantic love" which is nothing more than physical emotion or sentiment. Boy meets girl, he is smitten and loses the use of reason. Accustomed to hearing about "romantic love," you naturally tend to think love is sentiment and that contrition, love in sorrow, is an emotion. You begin to imagine you must "feel" sorry. Perhaps you have read spiritual writers or heard preachers extolling "the gift of tears" and so you concluded that you should feel so emotionally sorry in confession as to be on the verge of tears. But don't mistake emotion or sentiment for sorrow. These physical feelings may accompany genuine sorrow but they are quite distinct from it.

I don't mean to imply that emotional sorrow is necessarily false sorrow. Some persons do have a talent for publicly displaying a sorrow that is superficial. There is the story of the weeping young widow at the wake who was asked by her dead husband's bachelor friend if he could have some memento of his friend and she quickly perked up and asked, "How about me?" I have heard, too, of a husband who was so overborne with grief that he threw himself into the grave of his dead wife at the burial, but he remarried within a week. These are examples of spurious sorrow and prove nothing about the real thing.

There is an emotional sorrow that is genuine and wholesome. A healthy sorrow may overflow into the emotions and often cause physical manifestations. The important point, however, is that if emotion does not come naturally to you at time of confession, don't try to manufacture it. It is not essential to contrition. God may give you "the gift of tears" but He does not demand tears. Manufactured emotion is an abomination. At the present time there are too many people who are looking to religion as a stimulant that will induce a pleasing emotion, and many of them think confession ought to do the trick. This is certainly the wrong attitude with which to approach the sacrament as it adulterates the saving waters of penance.

The safe rule is to pay no attention to emotion as a conscious factor in penance. Let it come naturally if it comes at all but don't look for an emotional thrill or an emotional prostration. The sacrament may give an emotional exaltation or a "cozy inner feeling" to some but God may deny these physical pleasures to those who go searching for them. Seek first the kingdom of God and His forgiveness and all these other things will be added unto you, but if you seek other things first, you may get nothing. Those who use the sacrament for a psychophysical rather than a supernatural motive are using it for a purpose that is far from the primary purpose for which Christ instituted it.

This preoccupation with emotion in religion does a lot of harm. Unbelievers get the impression that religion is a narcotic, inducing a series of pleasant sensations to buoy up the fainthearted — and the intelligent unbelievers are not impressed. They boast they would rather live by mind than by emotion, and they claim that religionists try to escape into the cloud-cuckoo land of religious emotion rather than intelligently facing up to their problems. The agnostic says he would prefer to stand on his own two feet and wrestle with his responsibilities rather than wring his hands, writhe in guilt, and luxuriate in a peace-of-mind coma after absolution.

Catholicism deals more gently with emotion than does the agnostic intellectual. It does condemn *emotional escape* from problems but it does not condemn religious emotion absolutely. It says that religious emotion can be a great help to intellect and will, provided the emotion plays second fiddle to the mind.

Perfect love then is not a perfectly overwhelming emotion but an act of the will by which you love God whom you know by faith. You love Him perfectly if you love Him not for some selfish reason but for His sheer goodness above all things. Here you run up against the difficulty of loving Someone you have never seen except with the eyes of faith. I think much of the difficulty in loving God stems from the mental pictures of God that we form in our imagination. Some conceive of Him as "Baby Jesus" and the saccharine quality of such a picture stifles real affection except in the immature. Some think of Him as a venerable old grandfather, like God in the play *Green Pastures*. The trouble with the latter is that this old grandfather image seems to build up in our imagination until it becomes an oriental potentate who demands our homage.

Yet you have to remember that you will find it hard to love God without picturing Him in some form. The monk strives for an intellectual vision of God's glory, for what is termed an experimental knowledge of God. He knows that he cannot see God face to face: no man can look upon the face of God and live. But he strives for contemplation of the glory of Him who dwells in light inaccessible. St. Gregory speaks of contemplation as an effort of the mind to rise to heavenly things, a striving to pass beyond all that is visible so that sometimes the mind is carried away and takes its flight "above the darkness of its stubborn blindness, so that it reaches out in some measure to the infinite light, furtively and in an imperfect manner."[1]

Contemplation is the natural climate of the monk but it is not the natural climate of the typist, the office worker, the teacher, the doctor, lawyer, laborer. Rarely do they practice contemplation or even aspire to it. (Would that we had more mystics among us, but I am speaking of the factual situation.) Yet the ordinary Catholic making his or her examination of conscience in church on a Saturday afternoon does want to love God and to detest sin out of his love for God. To do so, he needs to have a more adequate concept of God than is represented by the popular images of God.

We tend to picture God in the skies, far off in the clouds, isolated from the world. This is pardonable in a child, but in this space age, adults ought to have a more mature concept. One recent scientific writer said that when we do finally travel in space, we will be disillusioned. Darkness will be all about us, we will see no clouds, no morning or evening; it will all be very unromantic and dreary. The heavens are not what we imagined them to be in our childhood. Theolo-

[1] Quoted in *The Meaning of Monastic Life*, by Louis Bouyer (New York: Kenedy, 1955), p. 71.

gians tell us that heaven, the abode of the blessed, is a place beyond the earth but they don't know whether it is up or down, near or far.

What we do know for certain is that God is present in a very special way on this earth. Our prayers ought to go *out* to God rather than *up* to Him. (Personally, I prefer prayers that address God as You, not Thou.) Our hope is in the life to come, but our duty, our human affections, our hearts are in this world where God wills us to be at this moment and where He wants us to use our God-given talents to help the children of God. We can easily love God at work in our world but we will find it requires a lot of imagination to love a mental picture of an old man on a cloud.

So Near Is God was the title of a book on the spiritual life by Father James M. Gillis, C.S.P. It is an old Christian theme. If God is everywhere as we learned in our catechism, then He is near as well as far away. He is all about us in nature. Elizabeth Barrett Browning wrote of "every common bush afire with God." And St. Paul summed it up in his address to the philosophers at Athens: "He is not far from any one of us: for in Him we live and move and have our being." It was no apparition but God Himself who walked the dusty roads of Palestine when He was here with us in the days of His flesh. Today He is still present among us in the fellowship of His followers, the visible Church of Christ. He is intimately present in every soul in the state of grace. Moreover, He is present in our neighbors. In the 25th chapter of St. Matthew, our Lord describes the Last Judgment and reminds us that He is present in the most unprepossessing of our neighbors: "Whatsoever you did to these the least of my brethren you did unto me. . . . For I was hungry and you gave me to eat. . . ."

It seems to me that you can attain to perfect love and perfect contrition without great difficulty if you take the catechism statement literally and conceive of God as being present in this world. This is a most important requisite of the spiritual life at this particular moment of history. For the great enemy of religion in America today is not atheism or agnosticism or existentialism but secularism. What do the secularists hold? They don't condemn religion. They tolerate it as long as it is kept out of everyday life in America. They want us to consider it "pie in the sky when we die" but they don't want us to bring it into politics, business, law, or any department of public activity. They claim that the First Amendment to the Constitution has erected a high wall of separation to keep religion out of affairs of state. In effect, they want to bottle up religion in the privacy of the heart or banish it to the void of outer space. So it seems to me that if a Catholic conceives of God as a remote Presence in outer space, he is playing right into the hands of secularists and at the same time removing God from the reach of our love.

In addition to the basic, positive element, love of God, perfect contrition also has a negative feature: detestation of sin. This, too, is something that is not easy to achieve at this particular time. For a sense of sin is something that is seldom found today outside the Catholic Church. It can be found in a few Protestant sects and in orthodox Judaism, but in the world at large it is considered rather "medieval." Ours is the era of almost unrestricted personal liberty. There are very few recognized ground rules for playing the game of life and in fact, very few people agree as to where the goal posts are. Certain actions are considered violations of the rules of civilized society but not of a moral code.

Recently I came across a succinct statement of the difficulty of developing a sense of sin today. It was from *God In Us*, by Miles Lowell Yates. Dr. Yates, an Episcopalian, delivered this as part of a sermon to Episcopalian seminarians: ". . . for lamenting our sins worthily, for being rightly sorry about them, we need a sense of sin, some realization of guilt; and it is hard to come by, in the midst of everyday life, when the issues seem so ordinary and commonplace, and when we can get away with so much, fix up so much, ignore so much, forget so much, and when it seems to us constantly that the *counters* are very largely in our own hands. Over and over again it seems to us as if we could affix a *period* to sin, especially if it is a secret and whispering sin, not an open and crying sin. Yet we can never affix a period, but only a comma – marking it off, it may be, from sins that may follow, but never ending its implications. Only God can take care of them; only God can affix the period. Only, I think, as we take in this realism, can we comprehend guilt."[2]

What is this sense of sin that Dr. Yates refers to? I don't really think we can define it, as it is one of those intangibles that are the product of a Christian life illuminated by faith. Some persons think of a sense of sin as a sense of hurting God. But if God is unchangeable, how can you hurt Him? The sense of sin is rather a sense of hurting ourselves by cutting ourselves off from God's friendship and favors. In turning our backs on God, we prevent Him from giving us His grace. We hurt Him in the sense that we bar Him from being to us what He wants us to be, a generous giver. By a good confession we take down the barrier that we put up against His generosity.

Call the sense of sin a sixth sense, if you will. It is an "instinct of the mind" rather than a cool, calculating process, something like the instinct of a musician who may not be able to express what is wrong with a piece of music but yet knows there is discord in it. This is true of a problem such as birth control. The average Catholic may not be able to pinpoint for a non-Catholic the evil of birth control in such a way as to convince him. To understand the force of the natural law argument against birth control, one needs to have

[2] Miles Lowell Yates, *God In Us* (Seabury Press, 1959), p. 90.

a Catholic "intuition" that comes as a gift from the Holy Spirit. For a Catholic sees the use of contraceptives as something that is evil not because the Church has declared it evil, but as something the Church has declared evil because it is a deformity of natural law. This "intuition" of natural law a Catholic may find hard to convey even to the best-intentioned Protestant. Yet the violation of God's natural law seems so obvious to the Catholic that he hears the term "birth control" as a jarring note in the eternal harmony, man setting in motion the forces that give life and then deliberately frustrating them.

Genuine detestation of sin means that you hate the sin you committed and shrink from it. This doesn't mean that you have to work yourself up to an emotional ferocity toward the sin and that you must feel perfectly miserable about it. Nor does it mean that you have to hate the person who was your companion in sin. Young girls sometimes imagine that contrition means they must abominate the sight of the man with whom they sinned. No, it means that you must deliberately detest not the accomplice but the sinful act because it was a violation of the law of the God who loves you.

This sorrow includes or at least implies a deep-seated wish to undo the harm that you have done. Occasionally some of the harm can be undone, as for instance, by making restitution of goods you have stolen. But in the true sense you can never really undo the harm you do in the sight of God, much as you would like to. Since this harm cannot be undone, you can at least look to the future and resolve you won't repeat the offense.

There is a type of remorse about past sins that looks like contrition but is neither sorrow nor detestation of sin and is actually vitiated by pride. The penitent is sorry but in a wrong sense. He feels like kicking himself for doing such a stupid thing as this particular sin. He regrets that this happened because otherwise he would have had a clean record and now that this thing happened, life can never be the same again for him. He wastes valuable time brooding over the past, detesting the sin not as a violation of God's law but as a spot on his clean record and hating it not for its evil but for the fact that it was a stupid thing to do.

He could save himself a great amount of wasted energy crying over spilt milk and at the same time experience real contrition if he would have the humility to realize God often works good out of evil, even out of the most stupid of sins. We have the old expression, "God writes straight with crooked lines," and He can write straight even with the aftereffects of sin.

Take the case of St. Peter. He professed to be loyal to Christ and swore that he would never desert Him. Yet when the portress accused him of being a friend of Christ, he denied it three times. It was, to say the least, a stupid and senseless thing to do after such lavish protestations of loyalty. But Scripture tells us that after the third denial, Christ passed through the courtyard, looked on Peter, and Peter going out, wept bitterly. Tradition has it that his tears ploughed furrows in his face. As a sequel to his sins, he became a bigger man than before. He began to realize how weak he was and how much he needed Christ. He did not minimize or rationalize his sin. He detested it utterly and the fruit of his sorrow was a greater love and a loyalty that was unconquerable.

So too, instead of fretting over past sins, you can learn from them and realize that you cannot rely on your own resources to fight temptation. Be sorry for past sins but don't fret over them. Be glad you have the opportunity to learn humility. Many a proud man never really understood what Christ meant by "Without Me you can do nothing," until he was swept off his feet by a gust of temptation.

This is not intended as a plea for "sin-mysticism." In recent years certain Catholic novelists have stressed this point altogether too much. They have given some readers the impression that sin is a mystical way to union with God. Through sin, some of the leading characters in these novels, although mediocre Christians previously, have become holy.

While it is true that God can work good even out of the results of sin, it is foolhardy for any Christian to enter into sin deliberately with any intention of relieving spiritual dullness and achieving a more lively awareness of the presence of God. That would be a sin of presumption and as irrational as a man who would pick a fight with his wife so that he could kiss and make up. Such a sinner would most probably continue in his sin rather than emerge from it in glory. For the simple fact is that the sinner usually commits sin because of the pleasure in it, and once having tasted the pleasure, he makes a habit of it. Each time he commits a sin he is making it so much easier for himself to commit it again and so much harder for him to break the habit. He may wear down the resistance of conscience so totally that he will never be able to bounce back into grace. The whole notion of "salvation through degradation" is a particularly absurd example of trying to justify an evil means by a good end.

Previously in this chapter I have spoken of perfect sorrow based on perfect love. There is also an imperfect sorrow based on imperfect love. If the predominating feature of love is a certain amount of self-concern, then the love is imperfect. I don't mean to say that we must squeeze every ounce of selfish consideration out of our love. This is impossible. I believe it was St. Augustine who said that we are beggars of God and that we are all selfish enough to ask Him to give us at least some of His goodness. As Schieler says: "It is the explicit teaching of the Church that love for God cannot be so disinterested as to exclude all thought of ourselves and our eternal welfare."[3] Always there is some element of hope even in perfect love and there is some element of self-concern

[3] Rev. Caspar E. Schieler, *Theory and Practice at the Confessional* (New York: Benziger, 1906), p. 80.

in hope. As mentioned above, however, if the concern with self is the predominant feature, then the love is imperfect. It is not necessarily sinful but simply less perfect than the love of God for Himself alone.

In imperfect love there are two degrees. The first is selfish but yet, we might say, on a high plane. We love God insofar as He is good to us. We love Him for what He gives to us or because loss of Him means hell and punishment. We have our attention fixed on God as a generous giver. There is, however, another type of imperfect love that is not really love at all. Here the spotlight is on ourselves and the perspective is that of our own selfish interests. This is called by theologians a mercenary love and begets a fear that is not a fear of God at all but only a servile and craven fear of the punishment that can follow sin. It implicitly contains a love of sin so that the general attitude is: "I would commit this sin if I could get away with it." This fear is, of course, of no merit whatsoever. It is altogether different from that fear of God that fixes its gaze on God. Summing up, then, perfect contrition is motivated by perfect love of God, while imperfect contrition is motivated by love of God because of His generosity to us or because of any good supernatural motive short of God Himself.

What is the effect of perfect contrition? Here we touch on a point that is generally misunderstood by most Catholics, or at least understood in a rather confused fashion. The point is that perfect contrition restores the sinner to grace immediately. This means that if you make an act of perfect contrition after mortal sin, you have your sin forgiven even before you step into the confessional. But, and this is most important, you must have the intention of going to confession. The perfect contrition, with the intention of receiving the sacrament, removes *the* guilt, the eternal punishment, and some of the temporal punishment. This is the teaching of the Council of Trent. Certain heretics, such as Jansenius, taught that perfect contrition could restore to grace only in extraordinary circumstances such as at the hour of death, a teaching that has been condemned by the Church. A glance at the essence of perfect contrition shows why it restores to grace immediately in every case. It is perfect love, and Christ said: "if any one love me . . . my Father will love him, and we will come to him and will make our abode with him" (Jn. 14:23). True, Christ instituted the sacrament of penance, but love is the fulfilling of the law and the law is fulfilled by perfect contrition and the desire to receive the sacrament. The theologians say this is true no matter how small the degree of perfect contrition. Obviously, the perfect contrition of a St. Francis would be greater than that of a mediocre Christian, and yet the latter's perfect contrition would be enough.

Perfect contrition reconciles us at once to God and it is not necessary to make an *explicit* intention of going to confession. All theologians hold that the implicit desire is sufficient since anyone who has real contrition wants to fulfill all of God's commands and that includes the command to confess sins.

The degree of intensity of perfect contrition affects the amount of temporal punishment that is remitted. A high degree of sorrow may erase all the temporal punishment here or hereafter.

Schieler[4] poses an interesting question. A person in danger of death must make his confession or make an act of perfect contrition else he cannot be saved, i.e., if he is in mortal sin. Since anyone may die at any moment, since we are always in some danger of death, are we obliged to confess or make an act of perfect contrition immediately if we have committed a mortal sin? The answer is that God does not require us to do it immediately. God is patient. However, if a grave sinner neglects to confess or make an act of perfect contrition over a considerable period of time, he will be guilty of the sin of

[4] Schieler, *op. cit.*, pp. 85–87.

contempt. How long a time must elapse before he will be committing a new sin by his contempt? Theologians do not say. St. Alphonsus says that the sinner must not delay the act of perfect contrition for more than a month. Schieler says that if the sinner goes to confession within the year prescribed by law, he will not commit a new sin by his neglect.

What can you accomplish by means of imperfect contrition? In view of the fact that most of us probably have only imperfect contrition in confession, this is a very pertinent question. The Church teaches that imperfect contrition accomplishes nothing outside the confessional, except that it might induce you to go to confession. But it does not pardon your mortal sins on the spot as does perfect contrition. In confession, however, the situation is altogether different. Here your imperfect contrition joined to the grace of the sacrament can bring about forgiveness. Without getting deeply involved in theological controversies, let me say that imperfect contrition must be contrition — however inferior the contrition may be. You cannot have the virtue of penance unless you have a conversion of heart, an act of soul by which you inwardly detach yourself from sin and attempt to return to God so as to be reconciled with him. (I am not speaking here of venial but of mortal sin: in venial sin, you have not turned away from Him.)

If your repentance is perfect, your motive is nothing less than pure love of God Himself, and God runs to meet you and welcome you back to His grace. But if your motive for repentance is something less than pure love, then you are approaching Him cautiously with something less than a desire for total surrender, and God will meet you only in His sacrament of confession. Some theologians (e.g., von Schazler) claim that the sacrament will purify your imperfect sorrow by enabling you to make an act of perfect contrition. At any rate, for your purposes the important fact is that you can have your sins forgiven by means of imperfect contrition plus the sacrament.

If you enter the confessional with no semblance of any desire to return to God, then your motive is not supernatural and your confession is futile. Luther maintained that all fear of punishment is evil and that imperfect contrition founded on fear of punishment only makes a man a hypocrite who still loves evil even though he fears the punishment of it. If the fear of punishment of sin is simply fear and nothing else, then Luther was right. It is not even imperfect contrition and is useless in the confessional. The penitent must have a detestation of sin along with the fear of punishment. As the medieval theologians used to say, you must keep your heart as well as your hand away from sin. But if your fear of hell is of a kind that really amounts to a desire to renounce sin and ask for God's pardon, then it is not hypocrisy at all, but a gift of God. It is an impulse of the Holy Spirit disposing you to receive the grace of the sacrament. The hypocrite that Luther referred to would want forgiveness without any work on his part, but the Council of Trent (Sess. XIV, Chap. 4) said: "Falsely therefore do some accuse Catholic writers, as if they maintain that the sacrament of Penance confers grace without any pious exertion on the part of those receiving it, something that the Church of God has never taught or ever accepted."

The fact that imperfect contrition suffices in confession does not mean that you should be content with this type of sorrow. It will suffice for absolution, but it doesn't show a very high degree of gratitude for what God has done for you. Therefore, the Church urges you to do your best to make an act of perfect contrition.

The catechisms usually say that contrition must be internal, supernatural, universal, and sovereign. These terms may sound technical and forbidding but actually they flow directly from the essential nature of contrition and are not at all complex.

In saying that contrition should be internal, the Church is simply insisting that it be genuine. How often we say "I beg your pardon," as we trip over a person's feet in the subway, when we really mean "Why don't you keep your big feet out of the aisle?" Spurious sorrow is very common, sorrow that is just so many words. There is no substitute for real sorrow; never, never in contrition. At times, as I have already mentioned, you may be dispensed from telling all your sins but you are never dispensed from sorrow.

The sorrow must be supernatural. That is, it must be based on some supernatural motive. You must be sorry for sin either because you fear or love God (and even fear of God imperfectly contains some love). If God doesn't come into the picture, then no matter how beautiful or intense your sorrow is, it is not valid for confession. It is not enough to leave the primrose path that leads to perdition, it's necessary to get back on the "straight and narrow," and that can be done only by fearing or loving God. For instance, it's very edifying for an alcoholic to give up liquor for the sake of his mother, or for a gossip to quit her habit of character assassination because she wants to be liked; but those are not sufficient motives in confession. They do not rise to the supernatural plane.

Your sorrow must be universal. This means that you have to be sorry for all your mortal sins. If you still retain affection for one mortal sin, you cannot be absolved of any sins. This is the official teaching of the Church and you will find it at least implied in various passages of Scripture and stated quite explicitly in "Whosoever shall keep the whole law, but offend in one point, is become guilty of all" (James 2:10).

Perhaps you may wonder why this should be so. Should not God accept what sorrow He can find, waiting patiently for total repentance? We cannot probe God's mind as "His ways are not our ways and His thoughts are not our thoughts." However, I don't think it's irreverent to imagine a certain similarity between the situation in which God finds Himself in dealing with a sinner and the situation in which our American diplomats have found themselves in dealing with Communist officials. The Communists twist and turn exasperatingly in negotiations. They zig where Americans expect them to zag and vice versa. They talk out of both sides of the mouth, one moment beaming benevolence and peace and the next moment threatening war. In somewhat the same way a sinner says he is sorry for certain sins and promises amendment, and at the same time holds on to his affection for a sin for which he is not sorry. How should God deal with such chicanery? Certainly He cannot absolve this sinner. He must wait until he repents of all his mortal sins.

Sorrow must also be supreme or sovereign. This means that the penitent must look upon mortal sin as the greatest of all evils. If he really considers it the greatest of all evils, this implies that he would submit to death itself rather than commit a mortal sin. This is supreme sorrow. This doesn't mean that you must loathe the sin with the utmost emotion of which you are capable. It is a matter of an intellectual appreciation of values. A man may feel more disturbed by losing his pet dog than by losing his home, but intellectually he would realize the home was more important to him, much as he loved the dog. So, even though you don't feel any great emotional love of God, you have supreme sorrow if you hate sin as the worst thing that could have happened to you. For that reason, we say that the sorrow must be appreciatively supreme but not necessarily intensively supreme. Yet at the same time it is recommended that you try to make your sorrow as intense as possible.

The general teaching is that contrition must bear some relation to the sacrament. This may sound rather technical but suppose that a man were to make his act of contrition one day, his confession the next day. Would the previous day's contrition be sufficient for the next day's confession? Schieler draws a comparison between baptism and confession. He says that in baptism you can use any water on hand even though you didn't obtain it especially for the baptism. So, he claims, the contrition that was generated yesterday can be used in today's confession.

Usually this is not a real problem. It is the common practice to make the act of contrition before confession or at least to make sure of your contrition before you step into the confessional. In fact, most Catholics seem quite aware that they should spend some time on their contrition when making their examination of conscience.

Once in a while an unusual episode might occur in regard to contrition. One day, for instance, a distressed young woman met me in the street and said she had just left church and that the priest in confession had finished saying the words of absolution before she could say the act of contrition. I assured her she was absolved because of the contrition in her heart even though she had not said the words of the act of contrition before he absolved.

If you are worried about your contrition, just look about you and you will probably find indications to show that your sorrow has been sufficient. Perhaps the priest suggested you make daily visits and you have been doing it. Or perhaps you have been avoiding the occasions of sin that bothered you in the past. Schieler offers Cardinal Denoff's criteria: if you approach confession haughtily, as though despising the priest, if you answer the priest's questions brusquely, if you excuse yourself and accuse others freely, if you treat serious sins lightly, if you refuse to use the means necessary to reform, if you look for an easy confessor with no intention of reforming yourself: then you have reason to be worried about your contrition. Otherwise you can be morally sure your contrition is genuine.

CHAPTER 7

FIRM PURPOSE OF AMENDMENT

In comparison with St. Paul's conversion, the interior conversion of a sinner may seem somewhat humdrum. Yet it is an exciting and heart warming drama that takes place in the soul of a repentant sinner. The first motion comes from God. He plays His mercy on the sinner and touches his heart, and the sinner responds to the divine invitation by turning away from his ugly affection and toward his Savior. The bad dream has come to an end, the exile is over and he surrenders himself freely to the love God offers him.

Your contrition for mortal sin is a many-splendored thing. When you summon your sorrow, you probably consider it a rather commonplace affair and yet it is iridescent with virtues. Hidden in your sorrow, even though you may not be aware of it, is your virtue of faith. The very fact that you make your confession means that you have implicit faith in God's existence, in the divinity of Christ, in His promises to pardon sin in the sacrament. Then there is the virtue of charity of which you are more conscious. You feel ashamed, or at least regretful about the past, and this remorse is your love in sorrow. Finally there is your virtue of hope. It gathers up your regrets and expresses them in a firm purpose of amendment in the hope of obtaining pardon. Of course all these interior acts occur simultaneously but in order to analyze the firm purpose of amendment, I will discuss it in this chapter as if it were a separate entity distinct from sorrow.

Your purpose of amendment crystallizes your interior sorrow. You realize you might fall again, so you make up your mind that you will do what you can to protect yourself against your own weaknesses. St. Philip Neri used to say, "My God, beware of Philip: otherwise he will betray Thee." Your resolve to amend means that you are getting down to business and making a doggedly determined resolution to quit this nonsense that is spoiling your chances for heaven. "By their fruits you shall know them" and you have decided that the fruit of your sorrow will be a resolve to do penance and amend your life rather than lapse back into sin.

The Council of Trent says that the resolve to amend your life is necessary in order to validly receive the sacrament of penance. This resolution to amend means not merely a determination to avoid this or that mortal sin but a resolve to avoid all sins in the future. When you return to God's grace, you don't want to hold anything back. "He that puts his hand to the plough and looks back is not worthy of the kingdom of God." Your purpose of amendment is your official notice to Evil Incorporated that you have severed relations with the firm and have no intention of ever returning. Now that you are reconciled to God and living in the midst of the family of God, you have every intention of staying permanently in His household.

Most theologians teach that you need not make an explicit resolve to amend in so many words as long as you have real sorrow. Obviously real sorrow necessarily implies a purpose of amendment. If you detest sin and have turned toward God, then implicitly you intend to amend your life. It would be unreasonable to demand from all sick persons an explicit statement of a resolve to amend. Such a person might be so ill that he would be incapable of planning his future. However, in the ordinary case the Church urges the penitent to express his intent to amend and this is generally done in the Act of Contrition: "I firmly resolve, with the help of

Thy grace, to confess my sins, to do penance *and to amend my life*. Amen."

By making an explicit resolution to amend rather than allowing your resolve to remain implicit in your contrition, you can make sure that your repentance is a deliberate, rational decision. Unless you explicitly state your intention to amend, there is a possibility that what you think is contrition may actually be nothing more than emotional excitement. You have read about the type of "conversion" that is often produced by a camp meeting revival. Highly emotional, accompanied perhaps by screaming, dancing, or pathological seizures, it is vehement while it lasts, but it doesn't last long. I don't mean to say that revivals never produce genuine "conversions" but I do say that those "conversions" are spurious that are induced by an hypnotic, high-powered preacher deft in the skills of mass suggestion. He clouds the minds of his hearers and at the same time opens the emotional dikes with his oratory so as to drench the swaying crowd in a wave of unregulated passions.

It is the conscious mind, however, and not emotion, that makes a firm purpose of amendment. You are not overcome by a wave of guilt feelings, you control them and you make your purpose of amendment after a calm, cool look at your sins in your examination of conscience. Emotional "conversions" are rare in Catholic circles and yet we do have to be on our guard against them. They are deceptive precisely because they seem so much like the real thing. Some persons living in sin have suddenly experienced a state of exaltation on seeing a beautiful sunrise or sunset, or they have been deeply moved in a moment of depression on hearing a childhood hymn, or perhaps they have been shocked by the death of a parent. Sometimes they are swept off their feet by the inspiring eloquence of a preacher. Such emotional experiences are not uncommon, especially among adolescents. They can be helpful and wholesome in themselves but they are incomplete as contrition. They are generally stirrings of the unconscious, but contrition must come from the conscious mind and the only adequate contrition is conscious contrition. A sinner may look up at the starry sky on a soft night and feel his soul has been washed clean by a "nature ecstasy" but that feeling is a bit too fuzzy to measure up to the standards of real contrition. Such an experience may be an actual grace, but God wants the sinner to make it the occasion for a definite, rational decision. The sinners' conscience in effect says to him, "Either put up or shut up!" In short, emotional impulses or unconscious yearnings for the good life should be brought up from the depths of the personality and out into the open of conscious deliberation.

Some spiritual writers give the impression that human nature rebels against the thought of making a firm purpose of amendment and they would have you believe that you must stifle nature in order to resolve to be good. The spiritual life, however, is not a civil war between your human nature and your good intentions. It is a war between the higher faculties of human nature — intellect and will — and the lower faculties — the passions. These authors sometimes say you should stifle your inclinations. This is untrue. You should follow the inclinations of your higher faculties, allowing them to keep your passions under control. As for these lower faculties, stifle them only when they get out of control. The passion of anger, for instance, if controlled, becomes moral indignation.

It is the nature of an animal to live by a biological law, the law of instinct.[1] The human person should live by a corresponding law that is natural to him, and since man is a rational animal, he should live by the inner law of reason. According to St. Thomas, your moral obligation is not to fight against self but to be yourself as fully and completely

[1] Albert Plé, "Moral Acts and the Pseudo-Morality of the Unconscious" (*Cross Currents*, Winter: 1959), p. 32.

as possible. The grace of God is given to you to help you be yourself, to fulfill the best aspirations and tendencies of your nature. We call this inner law Natural Law, and it simply means that you should be obedient to the demands of your rational nature.

You are yourself at your best, not when you allow your passions to run away with your intelligence, but when you give your intelligence (and will) free play so that your intelligence can know truth and your will love it. You can see, then, that a notorious sinner like Casanova was not a free spirit, but a man duped and dominated by his passions, whereas the martyrs were free men, free even of the passion of fear. You are true to the highest and best within you not when you turn away from God, for then you are unreasonable. If it should happen that you fall into serious sin, you are at your best when you return to God for, as St. Augustine said, "Thou hast made us for Thyself, O Lord, and our hearts are restless till they rest in Thee." You are following that inner law of your nature that points you Godward. And the wonder of it all is that it is God Himself who is giving you the strength of virtue to follow the inner law. Without Him you can do nothing. Your firm purpose of amendment, then, is a quiet, strong affirmation of the highest and best faculties of your human nature.

The firmness of your resolve means that the civil war is over; you are no longer divided by two allegiances — one to creatures, the other to the Creator. You have given a unity to your life and you are heading straight for God. Your soul is at peace. Inner tensions have given way to serene determination.

Your determination to do better need not be violent. The conversion of St. Paul came at a great dramatic crisis of his life but your situation is probably quite different. You consider your state of sin a serious matter but probably not a life crisis. You can make your resolve to amend, therefore, without any need of summoning up a vast emotional revulsion against sin. You are welcoming the Christ you barred from the door of your heart and He does not expect dramatics. He gives you peace and joy and newness of life for He brings with Him the Holy Spirit who is "the sweet guest of the soul," as the Mass for Pentecost says.

Detesting sin above all other evils, you are quietly determined to endure all evils rather than commit sin. No threat of trouble will divert you from God. But you don't have to be fanatical about it. You don't have to leave the confessional with a burning indignation against all the sin in your native city. Real moral courage doesn't usually bubble over with the crusading zeal of a Carrie Nation or erupt like a volcano. The sacrament of the Eucharist works gradually and almost imperceptibly within us, and I think we can imitate the unhurried pace of the sacramental grace. "Take it easy, you'll last longer" is as good advice in the spiritual life as in athletics. This may sound like a plea for apathy. I remember hearing a man in the street one day remarking to a friend, "Smith must be a zany. He never gets excited." But it is the zanies who do get excited. The best spiritual writers tell you that you should not expect to become a saint overnight. "The Lord is not in the whirlwind," says Scripture. My experience has been that genuine zeal takes the form of moral indignation but seldom becomes a burning fever.

Your firm purpose to amend is an act of personal dedication to God. Be liberal with your dedication and God will be liberal with His graces to you. The sincere Communist party member shames us with his dedication to the cause. His ultimate goal — the paradise of a golden era of social justice — is a good one. We cannot admire his mental dishonesty, his injustice, cruelty, atheism, but we can admire his sense of absolute dedication to the cause. Probably it is because of his belief in the goodness of his ultimate goal that he is capable of submitting to purges and even death itself for the party. Yes, his loyalty is a perverse and devilish loyalty but it is given in no piddling, bargaining spirit. It reminds us of St. Paul's great and liberal heart. He was ready to sacrifice everything for the leader and the cause: "Who then shall separate us from the love of Christ? Shall tribulation? or distress? or famine? or nakedness? or danger? or persecution? or the sword?" (Rom. 9:35.)

Perhaps some moralists might quarrel with the proposition that the purpose of amendment should be an act of personal dedication to God. They might say this is demanding of the penitent more than the Church demands since the Church only asks for a resolution to stay away from sin. This attitude seems to me to betray a sadly negative concept of the purpose of amendment. I admit that a penitent might content himself with a mere resolve to avoid sin and still receive absolution but I am speaking of what is desirable, not of what is permissible. I don't think the readers of this book are trying to discover how small a commitment they must make in confession, but how much devotion they can put into their confessions in order to derive the maximum benefit.

Why should your purpose of amendment be a loving act of dedication to God? Because love is implicit in the purpose of amendment. If you promise to stay away from sin, and if sin is the absence of love, then your purpose of amendment is basically an act of love of God. Does that sound too pat? If it does, it is because we are so accustomed to a certain negative moral attitude that we have lost sight of the heart and center of repentance. The negative attitude is that the moral law is simply a matter of staying out of sin. It arose perhaps in the Middle Ages when churchmen drew up examinations of conscience for the moral guidance of penitents. Around these examinations theologians developed a vast structure of moral theology. They studied sin as a metaphysical abstraction, charted, analyzed, classified it. They made sin the starting point of all consideration about morality. They studied theoretical situations and determined to what extent a man could be tempted without breaking the moral law.

We all know that the broad moral commands in the Bible need to be made specific. The layman needs expert help in finding out what his duties are in certain practical situations. The Bible tells him he must love his neighbor, but it doesn't tell him precisely what he should do or not do in his endeavor to show love for his neighbor. So the theologians draw from this broad, general principle the specific implications of it for the layman's daily life, explaining what must and what must not be done to or for the neighbor. Human nature being what it is, most people seem to fix their attention on the negatives. They think of the moral law as a list of *don'ts*, forgetting the *do's*. Morality, in their view, ceases to be love of God and love of neighbor and becomes a matter of avoiding deviations from love of God and love of neighbor.

This is why many modern theologians are challenging the negative emphasis on sin and insisting that the focal point of moral law should be positive, love of God and man.[2] Moreover, they want to get back to St. Thomas' perspective on sin as something that happens in the soul of a person, not something that exists outside as a code of penalties. With St. Thomas they would put the emphasis in repentance on return to God, rather than on the avoidance of sin. Just as your contrition is your love in sorrow, so your firm purpose of amendment is an act of love in sorrow. Your resolve to do better is not merely a matter of intending not to sin, but is a very positive resolution to give yourself heart and soul to Him in whom you live and move and have your being. I might express it in this way: sin is minus love (—), mere avoidance of sin is zero (0), virtue is plus love (+). You will never get to heaven by piling up zeros. You need the plus signs of love.

---

[2] See *The Primacy of Charity in Modern Theology*, Gerard Gilleman, S.J. (Westminster, Md.: Newman Press, 1959).

Do you promise to put up with any trouble rather than commit a sin? This is really what is involved in making a firm purpose of amendment. If you can't promise that, then your so-called resolve is hardly more than a lukewarm wish.

Now this does not mean you have to imagine all the possible troubles that might happen to you so that you can shake your fists at each one and say, "No, I wouldn't sin even to avoid that." For the danger in using your imagination in this way is that you might begin to lose heart. "Would I go to jail rather than tell the truth?" "Would I be willing to give up my job rather than give up this girl who is an occasion of sin for me?" It is enough for you to have a general hatred of sin and a general resolve not to commit it. If you worry beforehand about special sins and picture yourself facing the temptation, your imagination may make the temptation seem so formidable as to deter you from forming a firm resolution. You have to remember that when you conjure up a future situation in your imagination, you are picturing yourself walking into the temptation under your own steam. But when the temptation does actually occur, God will give you special grace and strength to fight the temptation. So don't cross your bridges till you come to them; don't visualize your possible future temptations. Simply make a firm general resolve to quit all sin. This is especially true of sexual temptations. A penitent can worry himself into a dither if he imagines himself in a cozy corner confronted by the glamour of a *femme fatale*. Probably she's not nearly as irresistible as he fancies her to be, but at any rate he's creating unnecessary problems for himself. So long as he makes his act of contrition and has a firm general resolve to quit all sin, there is every reason to say he has a genuine purpose of amendment.

The early Church was extremely rigorous in what it demanded as proof of a firm purpose of amendment. Often it would not allow a sinner back to the sacraments until he had performed for years rather extraordinary penances such as fasting on bread and water, wearing sackcloth and ashes, begging prayers at the door of the Church. The authorities wanted to make very sure that the sinner was really sorry and was not committing a terrible sin of hypocrisy.

We can be grateful that the Church is not as rigorous as it used to be in this matter of proving your sorrow after a fall. Certain heretics have claimed that a relapse is proof of faulty sorrow but they have been condemned. The Council of Trent pointed out that the fact of a man sinning again does not prevent his former sorrow from being real. We cannot always judge one act by the act that follows it. It is altogether possible for a man to have genuine contrition in confession and yet relapse into sin again after confession.

Now suppose a penitent *knows* he will fall again. Is it possible for him to have a firm purpose of amendment? I think the case of a drug addict is a good example. He may have the best intentions in the world as far as his purpose of amendment is concerned and yet he may know deep down in his heart that he will fall, that he cannot break himself of the habit immediately. Nevertheless his purpose of amendment can be good. For the Church does not ask anyone to look into the crystal ball and predict the future. It merely asks you to look into your heart at the time you make your confession and if you are sorry and sincerely intend to quit sin, that is all that is necessary for a good purpose of amendment. Even if you feel fairly certain you will fall into a particular sin, make your purpose of amendment now and don't trouble trouble till trouble troubles you. Take each day as it comes — and if possible, make a special new resolve about the sin each day.

Dr. Rudolf Allers,[3] however, says there are persons who have true contrition and yet cannot make a firm purpose of amendment. They are sorry, but they don't want to promise

[3] *Conflict and Light*, "Some Psychological Aspects of Confession," by Rudolf Allers, M.D. (Sheed & Ward, 1953), p. 71.

not to sin again because they know that if the same circumstances arose as before, they would sin again. Sometimes there is an element of vanity in this stance: a proud man does not want to promise something he may not be able to carry out. He dreads the thought of failing because it is a blow to his vanity. Or it may be that the penitent has an altogether wrong notion of what a firm purpose of amendment actually is. He may think, for instance, that a purpose of amendment should automatically insure a good life in the future. If this were so, says Allers, then we wouldn't need any sacrament of penance at all. The firm purpose would be enough to enable us to live a good life.

There are cases, however, that are much more complex than these. Some penitents refuse to make the firm purpose to amend, not because they fear the temptation will catch them unawares but because they fear they will welcome temptation when it comes. In these cases, the penitent might be truly sorry and yet incapable of making the promise. Perhaps he has prayed for strength to resist temptation but has failed, has struggled against habitual sin but failed, and now has given up the fight as futile.

This may be a very serious situation. Possibly the penitent has given way to despair and this is a terrible sin in addition to the specific sin he wants to avoid. He may give up the moral life altogether as he sees no point in trying to be good. Such a person would do well to consult a Catholic psychiatrist or psychologist. For it may take more time than the ordinary confessor can give, to discover just what is wrong. There may be a hidden factor causing the trouble, a factor of which the penitent has no knowledge. Dr. Allers discusses the vice of laziness as an example of a vice that may hide a secret cause. Maybe the penitent finds laziness his besetting sin and has given up the fight against it. Ordinarily we would say that a lazy man could cure his trouble by making himself work but he just prefers to be lazy. The fact is, however, that some lazy people are lazy not because they like to be quiet, but because they are vivacious, enthusiastic, ambitious. A schoolboy, for instance, who is apparently lazy at his books might be, as the psychologist will find out, not really lazy at all. He may be so ambitious that he is content only with great successes; and knowing that he will not be a great success at books, he doesn't even try.

Then there are persons, according to Dr. Allers, who are lazy at certain types of work because the job is no challenge to them. Or perhaps a child is lazy because the parents are pushing him to effort and he chooses to be perversely lazy, knowing the parents will bribe him to make an effort.

With many habitual sins it is necessary to analyze them very closely in order to find out what is the cause of the lack of firm purpose of amendment. Hasty judgments are hazardous here, as there is often more than meets the eye. The confessor probably has neither the time nor the competence to make such an examination of the person's state of mind and so a psychologist or psychiatrist is the one to help. Aiding the person to discover the source of his trouble, the psychiatrist is, at the same time, removing the obstacles to a free choice and assisting the penitent to make a firm purpose of amendment.

The purpose of amendment must be efficacious as well as firm. That is, a man sincere in his sorrow will resolve to avoid the occasions of sin as well as the sin itself. Common sense will tell you that once you are caught up in the whirl of the temptation, you may be unable to save yourself. But you should have avoided getting involved. In the hours preceding the act, you had a chance for a calm, clear look. You saw the tornado coming and you walked right into it. He who loves fire shall perish in the flames.

One final word about venial sins. The purpose of amendment need not extend to all the venial sins committed, nor do you have to resolve to avoid all occasions of venial sins.

If you have only venial sins to confess, it suffices to have sorrow and a firm purpose of amendment for one venial sin. However, you ought to have at least a resolve to reduce the number of your venial sins.

I believe it was the nineteenth-century British historian, William Lecky, who said that the confessional is the greatest lever ever devised for raising fallen man. The lifting power of the confessional depends to a large degree on the firm purpose of amendment. An habitual sinner may have the world's best library of spiritual books, he may listen to the most inspiring retreat masters, he may live in the atmosphere of a monastery. All these are only helps. If he really wants to shake off his habit of sin, he must do more than read or listen. He must buckle down and make a genuine resolve to amend. That is the first step on the road to sanctity. St. Thomas Aquinas said that you become a saint by willing to become a saint.

That's why the Communist boasts of regenerating human nature are so unrealistic. Communists view capitalism as the original sin and they claim you must be brainwashed of capitalism in order to be regenerated. In fact, one missionary, who had been in a Chinese Red prison camp, told me that his Communist interrogators talked glibly about the need of "confessing" your sins against the People's Government and then they went on to say that you must show your purpose of amendment by furnishing your questioners with a list of names and addresses of your capitalist friends. But Communism is not radical enough. It presumes the world will progress by altering the economic framework of society. The Christian idea is that it is sin that makes people miserable. You can improve the world only by going right to the heart of the matter, the sin in your own soul. Making the resolve to amend your life is a painful operation for the average man but with the help of God, it can restore health and peace to the soul.

CHAPTER 8

PENANCE AND ABSOLUTION

Absolution will remove the guilt on your soul. That does not mean that when you step out of the confessional, you will be haloed and ready for heaven. You probably have some temporal punishment to serve out here or in purgatory as a result of your sin.

You can wait until purgatory to serve out your temporal punishment but as the flour ad says, "Eventually — why not now?" Why not atone now for your sins and thus reduce the time you will have to spend in purgatory? Recently a Catholic woman told me of the various trials she had undergone, including the death of three members of her family in a comparatively short period of time, and she summed up her state as "All this and purgatory too!" I could sympathize with her in her plight and yet it is fortunate for us that we can serve out some temporal punishment here in this life so that we won't have to serve out all of it in purgatory. As an old priest-friend of mine used to say, purgatory is a beauty parlor for heaven. Nothing defiled can enter heaven and the soul is beautified by fire in preparation for the meeting with the everlasting God. And yet why wait for purgatory? The penitent saints didn't care to wait. They realized that even a lifetime of penance in this world is little enough and they wanted to do their penance as quickly as possible so as to be with Christ at the earliest possible moment.

Another reason for penance is that we are incorporated into Christ by baptism. If He, the innocent son of Mary, suffered for our sins on Calvary, it seems only fitting that we, the guilty, should share in His sufferings. We ought to reproduce His life in our own lives.

Now how do we go about this business of doing penance? Our whole life can be a penance, provided we offer up all we say and do in union with the sufferings of Christ. To live up to the duties of our state in life, whether we be parents or children, employers or employees, involves constant sacrifice. Just "getting along with people" usually means we have to give up our own preferences and whims. Any kindness you show, any pain you suffer can be offered up as penance.

Before giving you absolution, the priest assigns you a penance. He is imposing a penalty for your sin and at the same time he is giving you an opportunity to atone by saying certain prayers or performing acts of virtue or devotion. Accept your penance willingly—yes, even cheerfully. For the priest is asking you to take part in Christ's redeeming work and you are at the same time doing yourself a favor by cutting short your time in purgatory.

The acceptance of your penance is an integral part of the sacrament. If you refuse to accept the penance, the sacrament will not be valid and your sins will not be forgiven. But as soon as you accept it, you prepare the way for the absolution to take effect. Acceptance of the penance in itself is sufficient in order for the sacrament to take effect, even before the penitent has performed the penance. When you actually do perform it, then your temporal punishment is remitted (at least in part). I am assuming, of course, that you are still in the state of grace when you do the penance. If you were to fall into sin after confession and do your penance in this state, it would not remit any temporal punishment. You would be fulfilling an obligation but you would not gain any benefits. Like a person attending Sunday Mass in mortal sin, you would be doing your duty and thus avoiding a sin of disobedience but you would gain no grace.

The confessor will give a penance in all valid confessions. This is true even when there are only venial sins or only sins already forgiven. He will assign a light penance even to the sick and dying unless the sick person is utterly incapable of saying a prayer.

It may happen that you will make your confession and receive your absolution, then remember a sin and confess it to the priest. Some priests will not give you a second penance because the first penance can serve for both absolutions. It is different, however, when you confess only venial sins the first time, and then confess a mortal sin later. Then the priest will impose a heavier penance than he did the first time.

Some priests seem to give lighter penances than others. The Church has no sliding scale for the use of priests in determining penances. The general rule is simply a heavy penance for a grave sin, a light penance for a venial sin. I have met Catholics who seemed to think that the giving of penances was just a matter of priestly temperament and that a priest who is "a regular fellow," like the crooning clerics in certain movies, would always give a light penance. To say the least, a confessor who never gave out a heavy penance would be a very strange person.

What is a heavy penance? This is a question that has different answers in different countries. The general consensus, however, in all countries is that five decades of the rosary, a day's abstinence, or attendance at one Mass are considered grave penances. Five Hail Marys are a light penance. A confessor will naturally refrain from imposing a heavy penance on a sick person, even for a serious sin, and he may realize from the fervor of a penitent's sorrow that he does not need a heavy penance. Priests can use their discretion in their choice of prayers or practices assigned as penance. Some customarily give a certain number of Our Fathers and Hail Marys, some the Memorare or a few aspirations. Others prefer to assign a penance that will run counter to the penitent's dominant fault, i.e., fasting for sexual sins, almsgiving for avarice, acts of humility for pride. Many priests like to impose penances "in honor of the sufferings of our Lord" or in honor of the saint of the day. For instance, if it is the feast of St. Camillus, they might assign an unkind person the penance of doing a favor to a sick person, in honor of St. Camillus.

In the early Church the penances assigned were often very severe. Christians publicly guilty of grievous sins who refused to do public penance were excommunicated and were avoided by the faithful. Those, however, who submitted to public penance presented themselves to the bishop in church on Ash Wednesday. They were dressed in old, torn, and ragged clothes and the bishop put ashes on their heads. At home they prayed and worked, visited no public places and fasted on bread and water.

Father Alban Butler says in his *Meditations and Discourses* that according to a law of St. Basil in the Eastern Church, an apostate had to do penance a whole lifetime, a murderer twenty years, and adultery and impurities against nature were in the same category as murder. The Roman Emperor Theodosius once sanctioned a large-scale butchery of citizens in the Circus. Although the burden of the blame for the crime should have been shared by others, St. Ambrose, bishop of Milan, made the Emperor wear a penitential robe and live in solitude for eight months in his palace. At the end of that period he came to the church, knelt with the penitents and publicly proclaimed his sin. These stern penances were gradually mitigated, and the ancient practice of public penance had disappeared by the middle of the twelfth century.

The assumption underlying these rigorous penances seems to have been that a conversion to Christianity meant a complete reorientation of the convert's life. He was reborn in the sacrament of baptism and had become, as St. Paul says, "a new creature." Therefore, the early Christians found it difficult to understand how a person who had been raised from the dead to a new glorious life in Christ could commit a mortal sin. For repentance meant that he had crucified the "old man of sin" and had put on "the new man in Christ." However, the Church itself never had any doubt about its power to pardon. It demanded from the sinner irrefutable evidence of his sorrow in the form of penance but it never hesitated to assert its readiness to forgive all sins.

Why did the Church later relax these stern regulations in regard to the readmission of sinners to the sacraments? In his *Belief of Catholics*, Ronald Knox shows that here the Church has relaxed its practice but not its principle. It still requires a firm purpose of amendment even though it does not demand rigorous external evidences of this firmness of purpose. As to the change in practice, Knox explains the earlier rigor on the ground that a young and persecuted church needed high standards of membership. To sustain a high level of dedicated membership, the members had to prove themselves in a hard school. Knox has a good point here. The Church had to be much more careful about membership when it was only a tiny bud breaking through the ground than at a later time when it was a giant tree sheltering all the birds of the air.

Moreover, Knox points out that the Church dares to be indulgent today because of the vast treasury of prayers that have been offered up by Christ and the faithful for the Church through the centuries. These merits are used by the Church to help supply what is lacking in the penances of her members.

You will be wise to say your penance in church immediately after you leave the confessional. It's amazing how quickly and completely you can forget a penance if you postpone it.

The obligation to say or do the penance varies according to the nature of the penance, i.e., there is a grave obligation to perform a heavy penance but omitting a light penance would be a venial sin. I am assuming, of course, some deliberate and culpable neglect. If you sincerely intend to say the penance and it slips your mind through no fault of your own, then of course it is not a sin. In recommending that you say your penance immediately, I don't mean to imply a strict obligation. If you have some good reason for deferring the saying of the penance, you may postpone it. Penitents who make their confession during Mass often ask the priest if they may receive Communion before saying the penance so they will not have to wait for another Mass. There is no rule requiring you to say the penance before receiving Holy Communion and thus you can confess, go to the Communion rail and then say the penance later.

Certain penitents are so anxious to do everything perfectly that they enunciate painfully every word of the prayers they have been given as penance. Others say the prayers, then remember they have not formed a specific intention of saying them as penance and proceed to say them all over again after forming the intention. All this is unnecessary. As long as you say the prayers in your normal fashion you are doing your duty even if you don't form a specific intention. On the other hand, you can't cut corners with your penance. If you are told to attend two Masses, you can't get around it by attending Mass in a church where two Masses are being celebrated at the same time at two different altars. That would be cheating. Nor can you delegate someone to perform your penance. Pope Alexander VII condemned the proposition that a penitent could appoint another person to do his penance for him. Otherwise, you could leave the confessional and say to a boy in church, "Here's a quarter. Make the Stations of the Cross for me."

If you forget what your penance is, you may return to

the confessional to ask the priest, provided it is convenient and practical for you to do so. In most cases this would not be feasible. Suppose you have left the confessional and the priest in the meantime has been hearing other confessions. You flatter yourself to think he will remember your penance unless you have confessed some startling sin. In the ordinary case of forgetting a penance, make a guess as to what you think the penance might have been and perform it; if you forget the intention for which the priest asked you to say the penance, make a guess at that also. There is no need and no point in imposing a penance on yourself. If you do that, you might as well try to hear your own confession and give yourself absolution. The penance is an integral part of the confession and can be imposed *only* by a validly ordained priest.

The central moment of the confession is the absolution. All the rest is prologue and preparation. However, I do not mean that pardon comes only from the absolution any more than it derives from contrition. Both are necessary for the sacrament of penance. As body and soul make one person, so contrition and absolution together constitute the sacrament.

Sanctifying grace is lost by mortal sin and is ordinarily regained by absolution. There is no unpardonable sin. There have been heretics who claimed that great sins like murder and apostasy could not be forgiven, but the Catholic Church has condemned any such notion. Blasphemy against the Holy Spirit has sometimes been described as an unforgivable sin, but even this can be pardoned if the sinner repents. The Church assures us that any soul dead in sin can be brought back to life to regain the paradise of the indwelling presence of God. The fallen angels cannot rewin grace but fallen man can recover grace through a man who, in a confessional, possesses greater power than was ever given to God's angels.

Only God or God's delegates can forgive sins. The scribes were right when they asked our Lord, "Who can forgive sins but God alone?" To prove He had divine power, Christ answered the scribes by curing the man sick of the palsy. Christ was God eternal and all-powerful, and since sin is necessarily an offense against God, it was an offense against Him and He had the power to pardon it. Since He is all-powerful, we cannot tie His hands and forbid Him to delegate His power to another person. To His Apostles He did grant this extraordinary power on Easter Sunday night and today their successors, the bishops of the Church, possess that power which they in turn pass on to the priests they ordain.

A layman may be very dear to God but he does not have any power to absolve. Father Alban Butler notes that St. Thomas recommended as a practice of devotion that dying persons, when a priest was unavailable, should confess to a layman, but he did not claim the layman had power to absolve. The great knight Bayard, mortally wounded, made his confession to his footman. For fear of abuses, however, this practice was discontinued. It was conducive to interior humiliation and penance but its dangers were all too obvious. In *The Left Hand of God,* a novel, a layman under the pressure of circumstances presumes to pose as a priest because the faithful press about him for absolution and he is reluctant to disappoint their hopes. His compassion impels him to hear their confessions and he attempts to give absolution. We can sympathize with the plight of sinners who lack a priest to absolve them but there is a savor of Protestant theology about such a theme as we find in this novel. I do not mean that a devout Protestant would ever sanction such deception as that of an impostor priest but the episode recalls to memory the teaching of Luther, i.e., that every Christian is a priest and that there is no "special priesthood" enjoying unique powers. Catholic theology, of course, holds that Christ Himself instituted the priesthood.

According to Catholic teaching, the priest actually absolves at the moment he says the words, "Ego te absolvo a peccatis tuis in nomine Patris et Filii et Spiritus Sancti. Amen." (I absolve thee from thy sins in the name of the Father and of the Son and of the Holy Ghost. Amen.)

You have probably heard Catholics refer quite casually to "a slap of the ego te." When I first heard it, I thought it irreverent but I have come to realize it represents a deep faith in the sacramental power of the priest. It is simply an example of the Catholic's sense of humor. He takes it for granted that the supernatural is at home in our world. In his perspective, he doesn't see anything spectacular or dramatic about absolution. It's just a part of his life and he can joke about it just as the mediaeval plays used to deal in very earthy and humorous fashion with the facts of the gospel story. A convert who had just been baptized together with his wife, said to her at the breakfast that followed the ceremony: "We are not only admitted to the Mystical Body of Christ but also to a whole new world of humor."

Yet I have noticed that while priests, for instance, will refer humorously to something that happens before or after confession, they usually have a reticence about listening to or telling stories about confession. The obligation of the seal impresses on their minds the fact that what goes on between God and the soul is nothing to joke about. They allow humor to play about the confessional but they will not let it enter the "holy of holies."

The Latin words you hear at the end of your confession contain more than the "Ego te absolvo. . . ." They comprise four prayers as well. The priest says certain prayers immediately before the words of absolution and other prayers after the absolution. These prayers are, as it were, the setting for the jewel of absolution. In English the prayers, with the absolution, are as follows:

"May Almighty God have mercy upon thee and having forgiven thy sins, may He bring thee to everlasting life. Amen.

"May the Almighty and merciful Lord grant thee pardon, absolution and remission of thy sins. Amen.

"May Our Lord Jesus Christ absolve thee, and I, by His authority, absolve thee from every bond of excommunication and interdict in so far as I can and as thou require it. Therefor *I absolve thee from thy sins in the name of the Father and of the Son and of the Holy Ghost.* Amen.

"May the passion of Our Lord Jesus Christ, the merits of Blessed Virgin Mary and of all the Saints, whatever good you do and whatever evil you suffer, be to you unto remission of your sins, the increase of grace and the reward of everlasting life. Amen."

The penitent must be present in order that the absolution be valid. He cannot send a substitute. It is not necessary that he actually hear the words of absolution and in fact, some priests always say the words in a very low tone so that if they have to refuse absolution, those outside the confessional will not be able to discover it. Since personal presence is required, a penitent who would send a list of his sins to the confessor by mail or messenger could not be absolved. The very thought of such a communication opens up intriguing possibilities, but one of these possibilities is not absolution. Nor can anyone receive absolution over the telephone, as the general rule is that the confessor should be able to perceive the penitent in some fashion.

Just how close does the penitent have to be? That is an interesting question but theologians are not agreed. Many say that a priest can confer absolution only if the penitent is within approximately twenty feet of the confessor. Suppose a penitent confesses and then suddenly leaves the confessional before he has received absolution. It happens oftener than you think, especially with children. If the penitent can be recalled without creating a scene, he should be recalled. If not, the priest can absolve him while he is still a short distance away. In the case of extreme necessity, however, the priest is allowed to interpret this rule in a very broad sense. Suppose he sees a parishioner falling off a bridge at a distance. He can give absolution.

An air force chaplain told me of his difficulties during World War II in regard to giving absolution. Sometimes he would have to leave the confessional, or what served as a confessional, before he had heard all who were waiting on line. In a cathedral in Italy during the liberation, for instance, he had to leave the confessional to go to another post according to official orders. Hundreds of men were waiting to be heard. He therefore asked them to think over their sins, explained the proper motives for contrition, and then gave them general absolution in a body. However, and this is an interesting point, he ventured the guess that at least ten per cent were unsatisfied with this general absolution and would not receive Communion until they made a private confession to another priest. The ordinary Catholic is so accustomed to private, individual absolution that he considers general absolution a dubious substitute.

When the priest has a good reason to think that the penitent lacks something that is necessary for valid reception of the sacrament, he can grant absolution conditionally. If he is unsure that the penitent is close by, if he is not sure the penitent is alive, if the penitent offers no sins of his past life and the confessor is doubtful as to whether the acts he confessed are really sins, then he can absolve conditionally, prefixing the words of absolution with a conditional clause such as: "If you are alive, I absolve thee, etc." In a construction accident in New York City a few years ago, a worker fell into a cement bed and the priest gave conditional absolution to the unfortunate man buried deep in the hardened cement.

The confessor is like the Good Samaritan who found a man battered and half-dead on the road to Jericho. Pouring oil and wine into his wounds, the Samaritan, rather than kicking him off to the side of the road, brought the victim to an inn where he recovered. In his role as physician, the confessor pours oil and wine into the sinner's spiritual wounds rather than abandoning him as soon as he discovers he is a great sinner. The Church warns the priest not to abruptly dismiss a "tough" penitent whose dispositions are insufficient but to try to put him in the right frame of mind so he will be sorry. Pope Leo XII, in his encyclical of December 25, 1825, said that many who come to confession are unprepared "but are in such dispositions that they might become prepared if only the priest, equipped with the compassion of Christ, who came to call not the just but sinners, understood how to treat them with zeal, patience, and gentleness." The priest in confession, therefore, uses every effort to soften a sinner's heart. This benevolence on the part of the priest is a fact that is too little known and there are many fallen-away Catholics who, I feel sure, would make their confession if they knew the priest would not give them rough treatment.

As a matter of fact, I think lay people are more apt to be stern with a long-time sinner than is the priest. How often parishioners will phone a rectory to protest against a funeral Mass for such and such a notorious sinner whereas the priest involved is only too ready to give the sinner absolution and the last rites.

Sometimes, no matter how hard he tries, the priest will fail to persuade the sinner to repent. He will find himself up against the stone wall of a will hardened in affection for sin. Only rarely does it happen but when it does, it breaks a priest's heart, for he feels that he himself has failed to measure up to his calling.

Three principles stand out in this matter of refusing absolution. If the penitent is properly disposed, then the confessor must absolve him. Canon 886 of the Code of Canon Law says that a priest cannot deny or defer absolution in the case of a penitent who desires absolution immediately. God is willing to pardon such penitents and so must be the priest, His delegate. It might happen that a priest would want to defer absolution for some good reason but he cannot do so unless the penitent gives his permission. Second, if the penitent is obviously unworthy of absolution, the priest must refuse him. He would be guilty of sacrilege if he gave absolution to one lacking sorrow. Such would be the case of a man who would refuse to escape from an occasion of sin, or one who declined to restore stolen goods, or one who refused to make any effort to give up a bad habit. Were any confessor to attempt to give absolution to such persons, the words of Ezechiel could be applied to him: "And my hand shall be upon the prophets that see vain things . . . because they have deceived my people, saying: Peace, peace and there is no peace" (Ezech. 13:9–10).

Third, if the priest is doubtful about the sorrow of the penitent, he may in some cases give conditional absolution. In danger of death, for instance, a doubtfully repentant person can be conditionally absolved.

Looking at confession from a supernatural viewpoint, I would think the moment just before absolution must be a moment of breathless expectation for the penitent's guardian angel. As Father Alban Butler has it: "The angels wait in silence in expectation of this happy word; and at it, the whole court of heaven sounds forth the praises of the great God of mercies. . . ."[1] It was Jesus Himself who said that there is more joy in heaven over one sinner doing penance than over ninety-nine just who need not penance.

What does absolution do for us? If we are absolved from venial sin, we grow in grace. But what happens when we are forgiven a mortal sin? We come in out of the exterior darkness, put on the wedding garment, and are welcomed home to the family of God. As the Mass prayer has it, we "become partakers of His divinity Who deigned to share in

[1] Rev. Alban Butler, *Meditations and Discourses* (Duffy, 1840), p. 291.

our humanity." Our hearts are young and gay again now that we have shaken off the old man of sin. In addition to all this we regain the merits which we had acquired before committing the sin from which we have been absolved. I suppose most Catholics give little thought to this grim fact but it is a fact that by committing a mortal sin we lose all the merits we have laboriously stored up over the years. By returning to grace, we regain those merits. Some theologians say we regain merits according to our dispositions; the greater the sorrow, the more merits we recover. Other theologians say that we can be sure of recovering all our former merits and more because of our present sorrow. The important point is that we recover merits lost by sin.

What about the grace we lost? How much sanctifying grace will we regain? St. Thomas says the grace we regain will be proportionate to our dispositions but other theologians say we will receive as much as before and an increment due to the absolution.

A convert once told me that as a Protestant she used to love to sing hymns about being "washed in the blood of the Lamb" but that she never really understood what the phrase meant until confession opened her eyes. In confession, for the first time in her life, she realized the redeeming power of Christ's blood and, as she expressed it, left the confessional "walking on air." Yet I fear that too many Catholics have a legalistic notion of confession and fail to understand that the absolution derives its strength from the blood of the Lamb of God shed for us on Calvary. The lance of Longinus, says Father Drinkwater in his *Readings and Addresses*, opened the heart of Jesus to let something out and to let somebody in. It released a stream of mercy to the world and it let faithful and sinners enter into the Sacred Heart. Today it is not the spear of Longinus but absolution that opens the way for sinners into the Heart of Jesus.

While the priest is saying the words of absolution, the

penitent says his act of contrition. The usual act of contrition is short and simple as in the following: "O my God, I am heartily sorry for having offended Thee. I detest all my sins because I dread the loss of Heaven and the pains of Hell but most of all because they offend Thee my God Who art all good and deserving of all my love. I firmly resolve with the help of Thy Grace to confess my sins, to do penance and to amend my life. Amen."

It is not necessary to say a formal act of contrition such as the above, but it is recommended. The important thing is to be sorry, to detest sin and resolve to quit it. If you become confused and say the wrong words, don't worry. Remember that thousands of Christians have done likewise down through the centuries. A story is told of a Maryknoll missionary who was in a perilous plight during World War II in the Pacific, and who decided in his anxiety that he would say an act of contrition. He managed to survive the danger. Hours later, as he was thinking back on the experience, he remembered that in his mental distress he had actually said the words of Grace before meals. God was listening, we might say, not to the sounds that came from his lips but to the beating of his heart. The essence of sorrow is therefore not to be found in a formula of words but in your interior hatred of sin and your intention to amend your life out of love of God. Our Lord reproved the Pharisees, saying: "These people honor me with their lips but their hearts are far from me."

When you have finished your act of contrition and the priest has said the prayers after absolution, he will probably say something in the nature of "God bless you. Go in peace." If not, he will at least close the slide as the signal that your confession is ended. Once again, if you have committed mortal sin, the story of the prodigal son swings around to its happy ending, ". . . let us eat and make merry, because this my son was dead and is come to life again" (Lk. 15:23–24).

CHAPTER 9

TEMPTATIONS

A prolific source of worry and mental confusion for many penitents is the question of temptations. Some imagine that the very fact they have met with temptations is a sign of their affection for sin. This is especially true in regard to sexual temptations. Persons of delicate conscience sometimes throw themselves into an uproar by imagining the persistence of their sexual temptations is evidence of their fondness for forbidden fruits.

To understand the nature of temptations we have to examine their role in the spiritual order. Their purpose is to enable us to gain merits. As Job said, the life of man on earth is a warfare and therefore perpetual peace is an impossibility as long as we are in the flesh. We ought to let it drag on as a cold war instead of starting up a shooting war, but that's a point I shall discuss later in this chapter. However, we cannot win the crown unless we fight the good fight. If great saints like St. Paul had to meet with temptation, why should we hope to be exempt? God will not leave us high and dry. He has promised sufficient grace to carry us through any trouble.

Christ allowed Himself to be tempted in order to give us an example of the right way to meet temptations. His were different from ours in that His temptations were only exterior, whereas ours can penetrate right into the soul. Yet there is much in common between His temptations and ours.

It was, incidentally, a real person He was meeting, not a vision or a figure of speech, but the devil himself. Satan's first attempt was a modest request that Christ change the stones to bread, a sensual temptation to appease His hunger. Next He was tempted to cast Himself down from the pinnacle of the Temple, a temptation to vainglory and prideful display of power that we would call exhibitionism. Finally came the temptation to adore the devil in order to gain domination of all the kingdoms of the world and the glory of them. This was a temptation to ambition. His answer each time was prompt and decisive. He would make no deals with the devil: "Begone, Satan, the Lord thy God shalt thou adore and Him only shalt thou serve." Notice how the order of temptations is very much the same as that which we meet with today. First, it is a temptation to sensuality. If the devil succeeds, he doesn't need to go any further. The sinner will probably take up with other sins from there on. But if the devil fails to appeal to the passions, the next gambit is to try the penitent's pride: be yourself and think for yourself; show you know your way around and impress your neighbors, even though you're going in the wrong direction. If the appeal to pride fails, then the devil tries ambition. Many a man has kicked over the traces in his mad scramble for power.

Each temptation has its own life history and it's wise to study the various stages of a temptation to see where moral guilt begins to make its appearance. First, the evil suggestion is offered. Usually your imagination will picture the potential pleasure or profit as something quite desirable. It will represent the sex pleasure especially as a luscious treat. Up to this point there is no sin unless you have voluntarily created the temptation. Your will has not consented; and you cannot commit sin without consent of the will. The second stage is experiencing the pleasure. Often the forbidden pleasure will catch you unawares and you may feel the pleasure without actually reflecting on the fact that you feel it.

The camel has got its nose in under the tent of your soul, but you haven't become aware of it yet. The third stage is consent. If you banish the thought and the pleasure, you have won the fight. If, on the other hand, you willfully hold on to the thought and enjoy the pleasure, then you have lost. Until this last crucial moment of testing, your temptation has been nothing but a temptation. General McAuliffe was tempted by the Nazis to surrender at Bastogne. It was just a temptation. He couldn't prevent them from inviting him to surrender but he could turn them down and he did — promptly and decisively.

Yet, in examining your mental state, it is hard at times to discover after a temptation whether or not you actually gave consent. If you have a healthy conscience, and you manifested any kind of uncomfortableness or disgust, you probably did not consent. Maybe your fault was a certain degree of imprudence in not resisting the temptation more quickly. Sometimes a person will play with a temptation like a child with the neighbor's cat, holding back from it halfheartedly and finally dismissing it with a certain degree of reluctance. Since the temptation was never actually welcomed, the fault was mainly one of careless imprudence. If that was your case, you didn't really consent to the forbidden thought since you didn't snub your conscience and accept the pleasure. Maybe you resisted without enthusiasm, but at least you resisted.

When in doubt about your guilt on a certain occasion, ask yourself: what kind of conscience do I have? If you have a sensitive conscience, you undoubtedly would remember whether you consented, as a willful sin would strike you with the impact of a personal catastrophe. If you have a lax conscience, the probability is that you gave in. For if you didn't give in at the time, your lax conscience wouldn't be disturbed then or later. However, these are pointers that will probably be of use only to the lax, for they know they are lax and they can't deceive themselves into thinking they are conscientious; whereas the penitents who have a delicate conscience in their humility often imagine they are lax.

What is the proper strategy in the fight against temptations? First, you have to handle them with calm watchfulness. The accent is on *calm*. I don't think you need to assume a worried, fitful, fluttery anxiety about falling into sin. Nor should you distrust everybody around you as an enemy of your virtue, lying in ambush to seduce you. Such attitudes destroy your own peace of mind and make life miserable for all around you. Our Lord told us to be wise as serpents, meaning we should not be naïve and gullible, but He also told us we should be simple as doves. It seems to me that a shrewd, cautious, lynx-eyed surveillance of our neighbors might be worldly wisdom but it would not be the warm, open, genial attitude we expect of a Christian. One of the few times Christ criticized any specific person was when He referred to Herod as "that fox." An attitude of suspicion such as Herod's is not really vigilance at all but sour-faced cynicism, and it is not the climate in which virtue develops. You don't improve your spiritual life by imagining that every man has his price, every woman is a devil, and your best friend is only too ready to stab you in the back.

A calm watchfulness means an awareness of your own limitations, a certain distrust of yourself. St. Peter's trouble in the courtyard was not a lack of loyalty but a presumptuous confidence in himself. This is the presumption that induces the unwary to enter where angels fear to tread. Be especially cautious about your special weakness or predominant passion. If a gangster sends you a threatening note, you will probably have the common sense to ask for police protection and to bar your doors and windows through which an intruder might enter. Watch your weakness. It irks me the way some oldsters will bewail the way young girls in bikinis expose themselves to danger at the beaches, and yet these same adults who cast a cold eye on flaming youth will pay no attention to their own weaknesses. Some of them proceed on the assumption that there is only one Commandment in the Decalogue, the Sixth Commandment. So they ignore their own special weakness as long as it doesn't lead them toward sexual sin. Then there is the double-dealing lawyer who does tricks with evidence, the real estate man who lies about his properties, the politician who takes graft. They blithely continue to do business as usual even though they are sitting on top of trouble.

Don't get excited over temptations. Keep your Christian sense of humor and a calm, confident trust in God Who has promised you His help. Try to avoid that high tension which serves no purpose but to raise your blood pressure. As St. Paul says, "God is faithful and will not permit you to be tempted beyond your strength, but with the temptation will also give you a way out that you may be able to bear it" (1 Cor. 10:13). You have nothing to worry about as long as you trust in God and are determined not to sin. St. Augustine says that the devil is like a dog on a leash. He can bark at you but he can't bite you unless you put yourself within his reach.

When you are making your firm purpose of amendment, you might also resolve to "resist the beginnings." This is an old theological maxim and it is good common sense. Don't nibble at temptations. A fish that never nibbles, never gets hooked. Don't deceive yourself into thinking you can play around with a temptation and outsmart it.

Daydreaming can prove to be a dangerous occupation because it's then that you are liable to begin toying with an evil idea. You find yourself in a semiconscious state and all kinds of images form in your imagination. Gather your attention and focus it consciously and deliberately on a wholesome and good thought.

If the temptation is a temptation to neglect your duty, then the best method of meeting it is to face up to your responsibility. A novel popular a few years ago contained the underlying theme that a religious man does not have a true sense of responsibility. According to the author, who is an agnostic, a religious man meets a problem, takes refuge in prayer, relies on it to solve his problem and thus practices a form of escapism by shifting responsibility to a God. The truth of the matter is that the truly religious man faces up to his responsibilities, asks God to help him help himself, then rolls up his sleeves and gets to work. When problems confront you, therefore, don't give in to the temptation to dawdle or to stick your head in the sand, hoping the problem will blow over. Take the bull by the horns or, to change the figure of speech, bring your problem to a crisis just as soon as possible.

Most human beings, however, are more persistently tempted to sins of impurity than to other sins. How are these temptations to be handled? I would say: don't meet them head on as you would a temptation to evade work. If you try to grapple with them, the danger is that the shock of the clash will only inflame your imagination and you will magnify them. Sexual temptations like the limelight: don't give it to them. Don't give them your direct attention but concentrate your attention on something else. If you gather up your energies and fight the impure temptation, you may be able to repress it but repressed evil thoughts can be a source of future trouble. They will seek an outlet for expression and may develop into a neurosis. Rather than wrestle with an impure thought, forcing it into the unconscious, ignore it and let it starve for attention.

The important thing is to have a normal, healthy attitude toward the whole matter of sex. The sex temptations are part of life, evidence of the fact that you are a normal human being. Don't imagine they betray a deep sinfulness in your character or that they possess a dark and irresistible fascination you cannot conquer. Millions of Christians before you have undergone the same temptations and emerged unscathed. Today perhaps sexual temptations are more prevalent than in the past because of our frazzled nerves and the sex-intoxication of our time. But don't let your nerves or the sex madness around you disturb you. Hold on to your Christian sense of humor. That is most necessary here in the United States. Jacques Maritain has said in his *Reflections on America* that there is a world-wide preoccupation with sex today but that this obsession is sillier in America than in Europe because so much of it is presented as "scientific teaching" whereas in Europe it is just sex. One needs a Christian sense of humor to appreciate the sheer lunacy of "scientific sex."

Obscenity is in the atmosphere in the United States. Federal Judge Frederick van Pelt Bryan, in ruling on a book that contained many passages describing sexual intercourse in detail and with candor and realism, admitted that the book would shock the sensitive. Yet he refused to ban it since he said "it does not exceed the outer limits of the tolerance" which the community as a whole gives to writing about sex and sex relations. "Much of what is now accepted would have shocked the community to the core a generation ago. Today such things are generally tolerated whether we approve or not." Our era is obsessed with sex.

The novels, plays, and movies of our time present a source of constant temptation, as does the daily press. We have book reviews in Catholic magazines for adults, National Organization for Decent Literature, lists for children's reading, and Legion of Decency ratings on movies to guide us in our box office patronage of the cinema. Yet, in view of the enormous output of American presses, you will find yourself from time to time reading a book about which there is some doubt. The first step is to ask yourself, why am I reading this? If you have a good reason for reading it, then go ahead and read it and don't nurse a half-ashamed feeling that you shouldn't be doing it. If you have a good reason for reading it, you don't need to confess it in confession.

If, however, you find that the book is definitely leading you to the edge of sin, put it down calmly and decisively. You don't need to burn it or throw it out the window. You may imagine such actions demonstrate your moral indignation but they are usually signs of nothing more than emotion. Conscience is a dictate of practical reason, not a convulsion.

Moreover, when you detect obscenity in a book, detest the obscenity but not the sex. No amount of lewd and lascivious portrayal of sex, no abuse of it, no matter how depraved, can detract from the fundamental goodness and holiness of sex. Too many people allow their disapproval of unlawful sex to spill over into their attitude to sex itself. You ought to make sure that you are reacting against this or that passage because it blesses sin and rouses passions and not because it deals with sex. For after all, the sexual power is a power given to men and women by God to co-operate with Him in bringing into the world a new person made to the image and likeness of God. It is a gift of God that can become sordid only through abuse.

I might sum up the preceding suggestions regarding the strategy of handling temptations by quoting the very prudent advice of Richard Graef, C.S.Sp.: "The first of these principles, as we have seen, is that psychical processes, especially emotional ones, become strong by attention being paid to them. The second principle is that such processes become even stronger by our fighting against them. If we oppose them they become even more aggressive, and in this fight they grow. The more they are fought, the more they grow, so that this fight often ends in defeat. Even if we succeed in overcoming the temptation, we have not conquered it as a temptation, but have only suppressed it or dammed it up.

It will come back with seven worse spirits, and the last things will be worse than the first."[1]

Oscar Wilde is reported to have said that the best way to get rid of a temptation is to give in to it. Having been received into the Church before he died, Wilde undoubtedly regretted his quip (if he ever made it). Today there is a popular impression that Freud recommended the same method of meeting temptations. The notion is that Freud recommended giving way to sexual temptation since a repressed emotion may take its revenge by way of a neurosis. To be fair to Freud, however, we must say that he never taught that you should pamper your instincts. He insisted that your instincts should be controlled by intelligence, not your intelligence but the intelligence of an analyst. I confess this whole question of Freudian psychiatry is beyond my competence to discuss here but I think the notion that he promoted lust derives from the fact that (1) he belittled the conscience (the Superego), and that (2) he was hostile to any code of objective morality. He apparently had little or no contact with the intellectual side of religion and evolved his notion of religion from sentimentally pious patients and from the literature of the nineteenth century which presumed the religious man was ignorant. He argued that since conscience is unintelligent, it is possessed of phobias and foments a false sense of guilt that makes people miserable. He therefore advocated psychoanalysis by a competent Freudian doctor so that a guilt-ridden person could get a proper understanding of himself and return to mental health. Understanding himself, the ordinary person would then be able to control his passions intelligently lest a dissolute life of unrestrained passion get him into trouble with the law, other persons, and most especially the Superego which is a hard taskmaster

[1] Richard Graef, C.S.Sp., *The Sacrament of Peace* (Clonmore & Reynolds, 1952), p. 37.

and punishes offenders severely. However, the popular interpretation put on Freud's teaching is that he urged everyone to give free expression to his instincts lest he become neurotic.

The Christian, too, holds for the primacy of intelligence over the passions but he has in mind intelligence enlightened by faith, a factor that Freud never tolerated. To a Christian, it is precisely in the dark caverns of the unconscious that there is greatest need of the light of Christ. For it is in these caverns that the tornadoes of lust, ambition, and hate take their rise. In his *Pardon and Peace,* Father Alfred Wilson, C.P., makes some very pungent comments on the need of intelligence in the affairs of the inner life.[2] He notes that conscience is not a voice or a special faculty of the soul but the mind making a judgment about the rightness or wrongness of an act. Probably it is because conscience makes its decisions in a flash, says Father Wilson, that we think it is a voice. The decision, however, is the result of a reasoning process. To ensure the correctness of these decisions, the mind must be well informed, clear, balanced, unimpressed by impulses. For that reason we have to keep reading, reading, reading to inform ourselves on how to act in the shifting circumstances of our times.

Our minds should be fresh, alert, not stodgy. Says Father Wilson: "We are never too old to learn, just as we are never too old to mend." As soon as we suspect we have a wrong idea we ought to set about revising it. In another passage he tells us: "Beware of confusing conservatism with conscience, and manners with morals. Ideas are not necessarily correct because they are old-fashioned. We must keep the mind open to correction and to new ideas. Closed minds make moral and intellectual development impossible, and obstinacy and self-complacency inevitable."[3]

---

[2] Alfred Wilson, C.P., *Pardon and Peace* (New York: Sheed and Ward, 1947), chap. IX.

[3] *Ibid.*, p. 127.

It is true that, as Father Wilson observes, we tend to canonize the manners and fashions of our youth. It is also true that younger people tend to think every up-to-date idea is right. The teen-ager today tends to think his teachers are stuffy but many of his teachers think the teen-ager is brash. Probably neither is altogether right and the truth lies somewhere in between; but the important thing is that each should try to understand the other's viewpoint. Conscience is not a voice that never changes its tone. It is the mind judging human acts here and now, and the wise man knows that the principles of the moral law never change but that they must be applied differently according to the changing times. In the Middle Ages the Church forbade anyone to charge interest on a loan of money. Today, because of changes in the whole economic system, the Church allows interest, and even charges interest in its own administration of funds.

Freud insisted that a person needs the aid of another person, an analyst, in order to obtain a knowledge of himself. To a degree this is in line with what many spiritual directors have said. St. Bernard said he wouldn't mind directing hundreds of other souls but he would never dare to advise himself. Yet the fact is that the ordinary soul today cannot afford the time and expense of an analyst and I am sure the Church will never require penitents to go to analysts or spiritual directors under pain of sin. The Catholic idea is that the ordinary person can direct himself satisfactorily, though far from perfectly, as long as he tries to keep himself informed and free of the tyranny of fashion and passion. In fact, the penitent must rely on his conscience as his guide and he must follow it even if it happens to be wrong. Through no fault of ours, our conscience may make a mistake but God will not hold us accountable as long as we are in good faith.

When temptation beckons, therefore, make sure you give your reason free play. In sexual temptations, generally your mind will not have to delay very long. It can make its decision on the wrongness of the act almost instantaneously. "He that looketh after a woman to lust after her" is just as applicable today as it was when Christ first said it. In other matters, however, the application of the moral law may be a more complex affair. The main thing is to use your mind, not your emotions, in making your judgment of conscience. Some meet a complex temptation by letting emotion make the decision and later think up reasons to justify what they have done. This is perilous, as the tendency will be for the sinner to make the same decision in a similar circumstance and before he knows it, he has formed a habit of sin.

Above all, don't think of conscience as a voice. As Father Wilson says, "It is implicit heresy and logically applied would lead . . . to private judgment in the realm of morals."[4] The man who thinks he is following a divine voice within him, an infallible voice, soon begins to feel that he doesn't need an infallible Church to guide him. We ought to form our consciences by listening to the Church. I think it was Chesterton who said he became a Catholic because he was tired of thinking for himself. By which he meant that he realized how many mistakes he had made in thinking for himself and therefore wanted the help of an infallible teacher. Frightful harm results when a man thinks he is divinely guided, as in the case of Hitler, and his ignorance runs riot under his subjectivism. As Father Isaac Hecker pointed out a century ago, we should listen to the Holy Spirit within us. But we should check what we think are His inspirations against the teaching of the Church. We have to remember that Christ promised infallibility to His Church but never to the ordinary Christian. If the so-called inspiration, then, clashes with the teaching of the Church, we know it's not from God. It is only an hallucination.

It is usually said that there are three sources of temptations: the world, the flesh, and the devil. It seems to me that we

---

[4] *Ibid.*, p. 132.

tend to overestimate the evil influence of the world and underestimate the devil's influence. Admittedly, the world does have a strong influence. The old nursery rhyme had it, "Through eye gate and ear gate into the kingdom of the soul." The world pours into us through the senses, through what we see and hear and feel. Today in America we live in a democracy where public opinion is king and public opinion via the senses of sight and hearing asks us to succumb to the same temptations as the majority of Americans. Even our venerable Supreme Court tells us the climate of opinion in America is tolerant of acts and customs that used to shock our forebears. There is a hymn we sing in our churches with a line about "a world whose breath is sin." Yet this same partially sinful world is also full of an immense amount of goodness: mothers and fathers, brothers and sisters and friends, and all that vast multitude of good people and good things all about us. The world draws us to evil but the world also inspires us to virtue.

So, too, with the flesh. The tendency is to look on the flesh as evil and as a source of constant temptation, and yet nothing could be more un-Christian than to view the flesh itself as evil in view of the fact that the Word was made flesh and dwelt among us. There is a poem written in the Middle Ages, called "The Debate of the Body and the Soul," which tells about a dead knight lying in his coffin, apparently fated for hell, while his body is debating with his soul over the question of responsibility for their common plight. It seemed to me that the body came off pretty well in this debate and that the ultimate blame rested with the soul which had the final say even though the body's passions might have drawn the soul toward sin.

The chief source of temptations, as I see it, is the devil, and he is so successful precisely because few people seem to know he is around. Recently I read a story about a minister who reproached his wife for breaking her promise not to buy a new dress. According to the story, she said, "The devil tempted me." The minister remarked, "But you should have said, 'Get thee behind me, Satan.'" His wife answered, "That's what I did and a voice whispered over my shoulder, 'But the dress fits you beautifully in the back, too.'" Now I wonder how many people who use the expression, "Get thee behind me, Satan," actually believe there is a Satan?

Outside the Catholic Church the belief in the existence of the devil is gradually disappearing. The minister mentioned in the story was probably a fundamentalist.

The liberal Protestant attitude is evident in the recent book called *Demon and the Atonement*, by Rev. John Macquarrie, who tries to make the devil an allegory or myth. Macquarrie advances the notion that man, by giving his attention to created things rather than to God, enabled these things to become his undoing. They became a destructive force and this force is what St. Paul, for instance, meant by "the rulers of the world of darkness." On the contrary, the Catholic Church, in its preaching and teaching but most especially in its ritual, refers to the devil as a real person. The bishop on Holy Thursday, in blessing the oil for the sick, says: "I exorcise you, unclean spirit, so that you may withdraw from this oil and yield your place to the Holy Spirit." Fortunately, there are some non-Catholic writers who firmly believe in a personal devil and they are calling attention to the fact that he is successful precisely because so many people think it is old-fashioned to believe in him. C. S. Lewis and Denis de Rougemont, for instance, have pointed out how the devil hoaxes people by convincing them that the whole idea of a devil is a hoax.

Know your enemy and in this matter of temptations, your chief enemy is Satan. He does the disappearing act by having himself pictured as a weird figure with fork and tail. He knows nobody will accept such a mythical figure as fact and so he perpetuates the myth. The fact is that he has no stage props at all. If he does seem to take visible or even audible form, you can be fairly sure it's not the devil.

Keep in mind that Satan is the most negative character roaming around the world. His aim is to reduce you to nothingness and your life to meaninglessness. There are no bad things in the world as God never created anything evil. So Satan's business is to corrupt good things such as wine, women, song, and even nuclear power. He can't add: he can only subtract. He can't create: so he destroys. His aim is to get you to frustrate the natural law of things, to use them for a purpose other than the purpose for which God made them. You were made to function according to a divine plan but he tries to disrupt the plan. You were given the faculty of speech to communicate truth and He stands at the beginning of every thought attempting to falsify it. So he urges adolescents to sow their wild oats as he persuaded Eve to taste the apple; he does it by tempting the youthful mind to believe there are no wild oats since there is no objective moral law and each man can make his own code as he pleases. The upshot of it all is that he eventually tries to bring a man around to nothingness, to believe there is no heaven, no supernatural, no divine plan, no purpose or rhyme or reason to life. The last step is despair. He has won when he has convinced a man there is no hope because there is absolutely nothing outside the forces of matter. He is the happiest person in the underworld when he has made somebody miserable.

Remember, however, that the devil cannot make you sin. He can only tempt. All the devils in hell cannot force you to sin if you don't want to. I am making these observations simply because I believe that a great amount of trouble we have with temptations comes from the fact that we forget the devil is real. So keep in mind that when you are tempted, as St. Paul says, your wrestling is not with flesh and blood but against "the rulers of the world of darkness, against the spirits of wickedness in high places" (Eph. 6:12).

If Satan had a heart, it would be broken every time a priest gives absolution. It is exasperating to him because here the priest is doing the very opposite of what the devil is trying to do. Whereas the devil aims to disorder a man's life, the priest is gathering together the broken pieces of a man's life and making a unity of them. Whereas Satan aims to make a man a cipher, the priest restores the sinner to his dignity as the brother of Christ and member of the family of God.

CHAPTER 10

SCRUPLES

The word *scruple* has an interesting history. It comes from the Latin word *scrupulus* which means a pebble or sharp stone. A pebble in your shoe can make life miserable for you when you are on a hike and a scruple certainly can make your spiritual life miserable. A scruple may be described as an unreasonable fear of sin where no sin exists. A scrupulous person has convinced himself that he is in a state of sin and you can waste hours of time trying to convince him that his worry about having committed sin has no objective basis. You can tell him to forget it, get hold of himself and banish his worry but he can no more do that than he can forget a real toothache. The sin is imaginary but to him it is painfully real.

The scrupulous person is usually normal in most of his human relations but he breaks contact with reality when it comes to the matter of sin. In some cases, a scrupulant is sane about sin in general and has a blind spot only in regard to one particular type of sin, such as sexual sins. Of course there is a world of difference between a scrupulous conscience and a sensitive conscience. The sensitive conscience is healthy and keenly aware of the demands of God's love and law. The sensitive person doesn't want to offend God but he is not obsessed with a fear of offending Him; he is calm and serene. The scrupulous person agonizes under a gnawing sense of guilt so that the guilt feeling worries him more than the sin. Conscience in the ordinary person is nothing more than practical reason making judgments about the rightness and wrongness of acts, but a scrupulous conscience is anything but practical. It is the prisoner of unreasonable fear and the scrupulant is terrorized so that his ability to make certain judgments is paralyzed.

The plight of the scrupulous person is pathetic. In his examination of conscience he makes venial sins out of innocent acts, and magnifies venial sins into mortal ones or feels that he is perpetually placing himself in occasions of sin. He sees other men doing things that his confessor tells him are all right and which he himself knows are permissible but he considers them a sin for himself, as if God were laying down special harsh laws for him alone. He finds it difficult to take the advice of others on this particular point about which he is so fearful, even the advice of his confessor who, he fears, does not understand him. Sometimes he thinks he can discern sinfulness in a perfectly innocent act because of certain factors which he dislikes but which actually have no moral implication, such as smoking. He is constantly worried about his past confessions, thinking them invalid. He frequently doubts the genuineness of his sorrow even though the confessor has assured him he need not worry. His agonizing state is made more painful by the fact that other people have no appreciation of what he is going through and often aggravate his wounds by their brusqueness.

Now what is the cause of scruples? Some of the older spiritual writers were quick to ascribe them to the devil or to supernatural visitations or to call them trials sent by God for spiritual purposes. The most experienced spiritual directors and psychiatrists today, however, admit that scruples are rooted in emotional maladjustment. Because of the complexity and obscurity of these root causes, a scrupulous person can afford to look with a cold eye on any treatment that promises quick and sure results. Some supposedly "quick" cures in the long run only make the trouble worse.

With some persons, a defense mechanism may be at least a partial cause of scruples. This may happen, for instance, to a boy who is studying for the priesthood but is secretly afraid of assuming the obligations of the priesthood. Such a person might develop scruples just before ordination. However, his case must be clearly distinguished from those many cases in which there is no pathological anxiety involved.

Father George Hagmaier notes a number of situations in which individuals seem to be suffering from scruples but yet are free from any mental or emotional disorder.[1] He says that ignorance is often mistaken for scrupulosity. A person may be concerned about the observance of a nonexistent Church regulation which he falsely believes to exist. Once he is told there is no such regulation, the "scruple" disappears. National customs may make a boy appear scrupulous. A boy from Ireland or Spain may seem to Americans to be "scrupulous" on sex matters but that is only because he is used to a sterner discipline than is found in the United States.

There are times in life when temporary anxiety is not at all surprising and therefore heightened fears may arise that will look like scruples but are not. A deacon before ordination, even though normally unafraid of the obligations of the priesthood, may become temporarily anxious. The same may be true with a groom before marriage. It is not infrequent to find a well-adjusted woman overcome with self-blame on the death of her mother. This may look like a case of scruples but it usually passes off quickly and bears evidence only of filial devotion. Then, too, we all have our "blind spots" in confession. Some of us feel a compulsion to tell we missed Mass even though we knew we were excused by illness. So in these various instances described by Father Hagmaier, we have to be sure we do not mistake a normal mental or emotional reaction for a case of scrupulosity.

---

[1] Rev. George Hagmaier, C.S.P., and Robert W. Gleason, S.J., *Counselling the Catholic* (New York: Sheed & Ward, 1959), pp. 146–147.

Sometimes scruples are the result of a Puritanical education, and yet it is not uncommon to find well-balanced individuals emerging from very rigorous schools. It has been said that the Irish emphasis on the Sixth Commandment tends to make Irishmen somewhat prudish. It could produce that effect if the revulsion from sexual sins were not counterbalanced by an equal rejection of other sins. Then, too, wrong notions of God may be at least predisposing causes of scruples. If one thinks of God as a tyrant operating a world-wide espionage system for the detection of sinners, it is easy for him to develop a bad case of scruples.

Scruples are not an intellectual attitude of the spiritual life, a keen mental sensitivity to sin we find even in great saints like Augustine. Scruples are not a rational approach at all. A scrupulous person fails to think clearly because his emotion of fear will not allow him to accept what his intellect tells him is right and good. A certain amount of joy is needed in the spiritual life in order that the penitent make sane judgments. Scrupulosity means that fear has frozen the springs of joy.

The plight of the scrupulous is specially tragic because they receive so little help or sympathy from anyone. They are not likely to get sympathy from neighbors and often they get only rebukes from well-meaning confessors who don't understand their trouble. For that reason a scrupulous person should seek out a spiritual director and be careful to select the right one. If he wants to run the risk of walking into any confessional at random on a Saturday afternoon, he should be prepared for an occasional heartbreak. Not all priests will be patient with him in his pathetic unreasonableness. Today, however, there are more and more priests who are expertly trained in counseling and the penitent who is scrupulous would do well to consult with one of them for advice.

The counselor attacks the problem as an emotional one. Indeed the penitent himself usually suspects it is an emotional problem. Paradoxically, his reasoning powers are acute enough to tell him that he is unreasonable in his attitude. It is that paralyzing, unreasoning fear that grips him and prevents him from following out the dictates of his practical reason. He knows he is suffering from compulsion somewhat like that of the man who feels the need to wash his hands frequently even though he knows his hands are not dirty. So the scrupulant knows his soul is not soiled, yet he *feels* that something is compelling him to act as if he had sinned or is about to sin.

The theory on which the counselor acts is that we form habits of reacting to situations early in life perhaps between the ages of two to six. These habits are learned instinctively, become automatic and save us the trouble and time of making a decision every time we act. It would be a tough life if we had to deliberately think out every act such as washing our hands or walking down stairs. How do we go about forming these habits that are instinctive? Some we form simply by imitating our parents and doing as they do. We react to situations as they react. We want to hold their love so we do the things that we know will please our parents — and our teachers or other superiors. Even when they are absent, we try to do what we think they would like us to do. In this way we develop automatic habits of doing certain acts and avoiding others. When we are grown and our parents are not with us their images and attitudes remain part of us; and we try to behave and think as they would if they were present. In short, we have formed a largely unconscious habit of seeing things through their eyes.

What has all this to do with guilt? The theory is that we hesitate to disobey this image of our preceptors and if we do, some inner force seems to clamor for punishment. Some inner tension makes us feel uncomfortable. We have an unconscious feeling that we ought to be punished as our parents punished us when we disobeyed them.

Psychologists and psychiatrists seem agreed that we adults have a *conscious* conscience by which we deliberately judge the rightness of an act, and an *unconscious* conscience which judges acts spontaneously, instinctively, and emotionally. This unconscious conscience is the image of our parents and other authority figures whom I discussed above. It is apparently God's own device for preparing the child psychologically for later life. Provided we have a healthy family life and the right kind of parents and teachers we begin in childhood to do the right thing and avoid the evil thing instinctively so that good behavior becomes "second nature." But sometimes this unconscious conscience seems to go awry, probably because of the poor judgment and distorted notions of the parents who are responsible for molding it. If they were too rigorous or too lax, then the unconscious conscience becomes too tough or too soft. If too lax, the child's instincts become wild and undisciplined, as they have no check. If too rigorous, then the child develops scruples, fearing to do even innocent actions.

The result in a scrupulous person is that his *conscious* conscience will tell him an act is permissible but his tyrannical old *unconscious* conscience (or Superego) blinds his better judgment. All of us have had some experience of this. For years we fasted from food and water from midnight before receiving Holy Communion. Then the Holy Father changed the rules and allowed us to take water at any time before receiving. Many persons found great psychological difficulty in taking advantage of this permission. They realized taking water was allowable but instinctively they shied away from it as somehow improper. Here the unconscious conscience was working against the conscious conscience.

The priest who is a counselor tries to get the scrupulous person to talk about his earlier years, hoping to find out why he developed this idea that something innocent was sinful. He may discover that this person as a child received some frightening shock that led him unconsciously to regard anything connected with the shocking experience as wrong. But more often it is the continuing influence of stern parental attitudes which gradually forms the "apprehensive personality."

The counselor will try to show the scrupulant that he is not responsible for his unconscious conscience. It formed in him without his deliberate intent. Once the priest-counselor has helped unravel the cause of the scruple, his penitent will be on the road to recovery. If the person is advanced in years, the likelihood of improvement is often limited but at least he can learn to live with his scruple. The priest can urge him to say, "I know I can't shake this thing off. But I will treat it as an intruder and try to tolerate it with a smile even though it continues to point an accusing finger at me."

In the book *Counselling the Catholic*, Father George Hagmaier says that the phenomenon of displacement occurs in a great many scrupulous persons.[2] As children they developed a resentment or fear of a certain dominating parent or person in authority and they unconsciously transferred this relationship to the clergy, the Church, or even to God. It often happens that a boy will think of God in terms of his own natural father and if he begins to mistrust his father, he will also develop an uneasiness about God and what He represents. Such persons often know the right concept of God as a loving Father but unconsciously they transfer to God an emotional image of this person that they mistrust or fear. All too often a child dislikes a priest and falls away from religion simply because of his personal disaffection for this priest. I have read somewhere that Tito was slapped by a priest when he was a boy: his later antagonism to the Church may be traced to his earlier troubles as it is possible that he could not get the image of the priest out of his unconscious. Undoubtedly many persons fall away from the faith because the Church reminds them unconsciously of an unsympathetic

[2] *Op. cit.*, p. 155.

priest, brother or nun they considered harsh or unpleasant.

Father Hagmaier takes issue with a traditional method of treating the scrupulous.[3] That method was stated in a pamphlet published in 1932 entitled *Are You Scrupulous?* which was written by Rev. Daniel A. Lord, S.J., and Rev. Francis J. O'Boyle, S.J. The pamphlet asserts that scrupulous persons must be made to realize that they have a false conscience and therefore they must substitute the conscience of the confessor. The implication is that scruples are an ailment of the conscience, conscience being the intellect judging the rightness or wrongness of an act. But the fact is that there is usually nothing wrong with a scrupulant's conscience in itself. The trouble is emotional. He is capable of making correct judgments about other people's actions, he knows what is objectively right or wrong, but the emotion of fear paralyzes him and prevents him from applying his correct conclusions to himself with any degree of comfort. He *knows* he is not guilty — that is the judgment of his conscience — but he *feels* guilty.

Therefore it is highly dubious to recommend that the penitent adopt the conscience of the priest, with the penitent having no other duty than to obey the priest. He needs to develop a sense of initiative to fight against his fears and to stand on his own two feet with self-assurance. Blind obedience, says Father Hagmaier, works with some penitents but more often than not, the penitent is not satisfied with it. Often he goes from one confessor to another until he finds one who, he thinks, will understand him.

In many cases, however, the priest cannot understand him because the priest is too ready to judge that all scrupulous people are alike and that the quick formula of ready obedience will solve every case. But seldom does blind obedience dispel fear, the sources of which are deep in the unconscious.

Is there nothing then that the scrupulous person can do

[3] *Op. cit.*, p. 156.

short of a visit to a psychiatrist? If the case is serious and far advanced, the aid of a psychiatrist is to be warmly recommended. But the distress of many penitents is not acute enough to require psychiatric help. With these the priest can be of considerable help in listening patiently and at length to the scrupulant and showing sympathy and as much understanding as he can muster. He can be of great help if he is skilled in counseling and is willing to give the sufferer his time over a long period. Ideally, the priest should see the penitent outside the confessional since the trouble is an emotional and not a moral problem. In these sessions the penitent will unburden himself frankly and honestly, answering the priest's questions when necessary, and going back into his childhood memories to discover the cause of the trouble. It is very important for the penitent to describe his reactions to his parents and teachers and priests. Unpleasant personal relationships in childhood, as I mentioned above, are often transferred in later life to the Church and to God.

If you suffer from scruples, you can help yourself by constantly reminding yourself that your trouble comes not from your deliberate moral choice but from your emotions. Rest assured that hundreds of other people have the same trouble as yourself and that you are not an evil person. You are suffering not from guilt but from a *feeling* of guilt which you have not caused. So while your mind tells you that you are not to blame, your emotions gnaw at you. It will ease your distress, however, to know that God is not displeased with you and, after all, that is what counts. Your heart is in the right place even though your compulsive fears may be out of order.

So the next time this brooding anxiety comes over you, try to give these worries no more importance than they deserve. Or if this guilt feeling is an abiding condition, perhaps you can learn to adjust yourself to it as you would adapt yourself to a hearing defect or some other physical ailment.

For this is an essentially emotional, not a moral problem, and when the fear starts acting up, just say to yourself that painful as it may be, this feeling has nothing to do with your relationship to God. As a free being, your relation to Him depends upon your freely given love, not on your jitters. You can be blamed for committing a coldly premeditated and deliberate sin but you can't be blamed for this anxiety. Your trouble can probably be cured but it will take time. Meanwhile live with it as cheerfully and hopefully as you can. At the same time, stand up to your fear and talk it down, make decisions in the face of it. Above all, seek the professional counsel you need.

In confessing sexual sins, you need not press the priest to find out if he has heard every word and has understood exactly what you are trying to say. He wants to get you safely through this squall and besides he has been instructed not to question on sex matters too closely. The Church has told him that a generalized confession of sexual sins is better than a full and complete confession of all colorful details. If he gives you a light penance, don't take that to mean that he has misunderstood what you said. He knows you don't deserve a heavy penance. Above all, go to Communion without qualms if you wish. If Holy Communion brings you peace and consolation, do not let your fears deprive you of these blessings. And in your daily life, feel safe in doing what ordinary Christians do. Our Lord has not demanded a higher standard of you than of his millions of other Christians. Remember that He said His yoke is sweet and His burden light.

CHAPTER 11

SPECIAL PROBLEMS

Children's Confessions

One of the perplexing problems connected with Catholic education is the problem of children's confessions. The general practice in our schools is to dismiss the children at a certain hour and march them over to the church where a number of priests will be on hand to hear their confessions. This arrangement has its drawbacks and critics can be heard complaining about "herding" the children for "assembly-line confessions" and "push-button absolutions." It is a complicated problem that admits of no simple solution.

There is, however, a real danger that regimented confessions may cause children to regard confession as a routine event in the day's schedule and the natural result will be that they will confess mechanically. Moreover there is the possibility that they will make bad confessions. If a child has committed what he considers a mortal sin, if he knows the confessor and fears what his classmates might say if he makes himself conspicuous by staying out of the confessional, he will be tempted to conceal the sin in his confession.

I do not presume to inform teaching sisters and brothers how to prepare children for confession, as they know far more about it than I. But I do think it might be helpful to offer some suggestions to parents. They ought to be specially interested in helping to form right confessional habits in their youngsters because confession does play a large role in the developing religious life of the child. These childhood encounters with priests at close range may prove to be crucial moments in a child's life. Forming right habits now may nip wrong practices in the bud, practices that might spell disaster for the child's religious life later on.

While the parent ought to explain to the child the need of an examination of conscience before confession, I would not recommend giving the child a printed formula of examination of conscience. Such formulas are usually beyond the child's comprehension as they are generally phrased in pietistic or theological language that puzzles him. Sometimes the language traps him in amusing situations (e.g., a tot confessing the sin of adultery) that might cause him to develop a wrong attitude to the sacrament.

Without giving the child the impression that God watches him hawklike, ready to pounce on him for hiding a sin in confession, a parent can remind the child that God already knows the sins he has committed. The important thing is not to narrow the child's concept of the scope of God's knowledge but to widen his perspective on God's love.

Today, stealing seems to be a general practice among children. Whether it is more prevalent than in other generations, I don't know — but the fact is that children seem to think little of filching candy bars in five-and-ten-cent stores, picking up "souvenirs" in hotels and keeping the change when mother sends them to the store for groceries. The parent can gently explain to the child that theft is the stealing of any form of property that belongs to another and that God sees all thefts.

Parents should encourage the child to be frank and open in confessing to the priest. I don't believe they should pry into the child's secrets but they should try to persuade the child to be utterly honest. An honest and straightforward youngster will reveal facts that the priest may find very helpful. For instance, it may be that the child is very much under the sinister influence of an older boy. If the child knows the priest is sympathetic and understanding, he will open up, telling him even things he will not tell his parents.

Again, the parent can be helpful to the child in explaining what it means to be sorry. Contrition is a very important part of confession and I suspect that children's confessions are sometimes doubtfully valid because of lack of sorrow. I don't mean that the confessions are deliberately bad confessions in which the child refuses to feel sorry for sins but rather that the child makes a routine confession without remembering to feel sorry. Usually there is genuine sorrow in the heart of the child. It is waiting to be tapped. The parent can help him to tap this sorrow. Rarely will you find that type of precocious juvenile monster who has hardened his heart even before he has reached his teens.

What about impurity? Every parent knows we are living in a sex-obsessed age. Children are living under a constant barrage of temptations impinging on their sense of sight and hearing almost every hour of the day. What is the parent to do? He must respect the privacy of the child. He cannot be probing into his secret thoughts and his every action in order to discover whether the child is committing secret sins. The earnest parent is baffled. He knows that sins of impurity are rife among adolescents but he feels thwarted as far as helping his own children is concerned.

He can at least continue to instruct the child in right concepts of sex, explaining to him that it is a God-given instinct that must be cherished carefully until it may be used in accordance with God's precepts in the married state. Second, I think the parent can help keep an eye on those emotional states in a child that conduce to sins of impurity. Adolescence is a stormy time for the growing boy or girl. As they emerge from the serenity and relative security of childhood, they sail out into the swirling seas of teen-age problems. A boy may feel unwanted and perhaps inadequate and these feelings may induce him to take brief moments of consolation in sexual pleasure. In his mixed-up state, constant thwarting by parents will only make him more miserable and more ready to commit sins, especially if his daytime hours are spent with sex-minded confreres, TV, and "girlie" magazines.

What I am saying is simply that psychological factors are often the predisposing causes of secret impurities. To be specific, the parent can watch the adolescent's habits of daydreaming. In itself it is not a bad habit. I suppose most every great man was a daydreamer. They are often, as Arthur O'Shaughnessy says in his poem, "the movers and shakers of the world forever it seems." But there is a point beyond which daydreaming becomes unhealthy, the next door to sin. The parent can attempt to direct the child into healthy contacts with other adolescents and perhaps into amusements or occupations in which the child will begin to forget his sense of frustration or depression. In so doing the parent can help to prevent his child from committing sins of impurity and perhaps at the same time help save him from the sacrilege of making a bad confession.

Some parents seem to feel that they need not concern themselves about their children's confessions in the vacation months. Sad to say, many Catholic children never enter the confessional during the summer. They have been relieved of school discipline that got them to confession once a month and in summer they do not go at all. Vacation months, however, can be a wonderful opportunity for parents not only to keep their children faithful to regular confession but also to help them make fervent and deliberate confessions freely and on their own initiative. Habits that are formed freely last longer than those that are formed under pressure of discipline and in accordance with routine. So I would recommend that parents make a special effort to encourage children to go to confession in the vacation months. Let the children go by themselves. Let them find out on their own the satisfaction that comes from making a good confession.

Confessions of the Sick

The confession of a sick person often becomes more of a problem for members of his family than for the sick person himself. Today families often show a false solicitude for the sick member. Fearing to disturb the patient's peace of mind, they postpone asking the priest to visit him in the hospital. They intend to call the priest at a later time when the patient will be more at ease. This is not a common problem in Catholic hospitals but it is definitely a real problem in nonsectarian hospitals. And even in devout families you will encounter this reluctance to summon a priest, especially among those who seem to have an old-world notion that the appearance of the priest is the sure sign of the approaching end.

Families that defer the priest's visit are often encouraged in their stand by doctors at non-Catholic hospitals. The latter may actually be well disposed to the Church but they are unaware of the importance of the sacraments and supremely anxious to shield the patient from anything that might prove psychologically disturbing. This seems to be more true of the older physicians than of the younger doctors who are apt to appreciate the relation between religion and health. But the fact is that only rarely today does the appearance of the priest at the bedside disturb the patient. It would be closer to the truth to say that the opposite is generally true. Even in minor illnesses, the ordinary Catholic patient wants to see the priest immediately and will not hesitate to criticize the hospital authorities or the priest himself if he does not receive the usual priestly ministrations. It is such a regular feature of hospital routine that the patient expects it as a matter of course.

If a priest is bound to hear the confessions of those in danger of death even at a risk to his own life, if a priest will interrupt Mass (no other priest being available) to attend a dying man, then surely the relatives should not dismiss lightly their duty to request this spiritual work of mercy. Even when the sick man is on his way to the operating room, some families still dally and talk about "having the priest if he takes a bad turn." But death has a habit of arriving unexpectedly, and even if the patient survives the operation, he may be so mentally confused as to be unable to make a complete confession.

There are times when the patient himself will ask the priest to postpone the confession. The family ought not to welcome this move or at least they should not accede to it for more than a day. They should try to persuade the sick person to confess as soon as possible. They and the priest can assure him that if he is worried about making a full confession, the priest will help him with his examination of conscience. Needless to say, in cases of obstinate refusal from the patient, the family should pray fervently to the Holy Spirit to give the sick man grace to change his mind. This is especially necessary when the family knows that the sick man has been involved in a bad marriage.

Someone may comment on the above remarks with the observation that we must respect the wishes of the sick person and that we should not force religious ministrations upon him unless he expresses a desire for them in no uncertain tone. No priest is going to use physical force on the patient but he should — and the family should — use the arts of persuasion to get the patient to make his confession. If he stubbornly refuses to submit to a necessary operation or medical treatment or transfusion, the doctor will certainly attempt to persuade him to see his error. Why should not the family do likewise in regard to sacramental help? They would co-operate with the doctor in urging the transfusion. Why not co-operate with the priest in urging the confession?

The patient's intention, it seems to me, should not be judged by his mood of the moment which may give rise to some very fuzzy thinking due to his physical condition. At this moment he may be so preoccupied with his physical pain that he is unable to do any concentrated thinking about religion. But his abiding intent can be judged by the general tenor of his past life. If he has lived as a Catholic, if he has received the sacraments, even if he has committed serious sins, we have good reason to presume he would want to die reconciled to his God. He is a member of the Church and entitled to the privileges of membership, especially the sacraments, and he should not be presumed to renounce them unless he has done so explicitly and definitively; and even here we can hope against hope. Remember the old English verse: "Betwixt the stirrup and the ground; Mercy I asked; mercy I found."

By all means be solicitous for the sick, help them with medicines and skilled physicians and the facilities of modern hospitals; but remember that the sacraments are quite as necessary as the corporal works of mercy.

General Confessions

A general confession is the repetition of previous confessions, whether it be some or all of the previous confessions. A general confession should be made when you are morally certain that some of your previous confessions were bad. It should not of course be made when the repetition of the old confessions would only do you harm. This frequently happens with scrupulous persons who repeat and repeat confessions and succeed only in increasing their anxieties. Apart from the above two situations, you may make a general confession if you honestly think that a general confession would help you in some way.

A dying person, of course, may make a general confession if he is in possession of his faculties. Those who are entering into a new state of life are urged to make a general confession. A young man or woman entering religious life or a couple about to be married do well to signalize the new step by making a review of their past lives. This may help them to become more co-operative with God's graces in the new way of life. Sometimes those about to marry are worried about sins that happened during courtship. Even though they have been absolved, they seem to feel that God may not bless their marriage because they have not prepared for it properly. By making a general confession they can bring home to themselves the fact that God has forgiven the past and is ready to give them fresh and wonderful graces in the sacrament they are about to receive. Marital life will be hard enough for them without having to worry about clouds hanging over them from the past. A new broom sweeps clean and a new sacrament can perform wonders provided memories of the past don't keep breaking into the present.

You may be disturbed by memories of a bad confession made in the dim past. Maybe you have been paying no attention to the invalid confession until you make a mission or retreat — and suddenly remember some mortal sin you concealed in the confession either from shame or timidity. This does not mean that all your confessions have been bad. Suppose you concealed a serious sin in a confession when you were a child. Then perhaps the matter left your mind and all these intervening years you have been making contrite confessions in all honesty, forgetting the bad confession. The priest has been forgiving your sins (even those you forgot to tell); but nevertheless you may want to make a general confession for the sake of your own peace of mind. For although your sins have been forgiven, you have an obligation to tell the forgotten sin as soon as you remember it. The rule is that the priest's absolution pardons all your sins — even those you forget to tell — provided you intend to tell all. But you do have an obligation to confess forgotten sins in your next confession, or as soon as you remember them. In brief, you *must* confess the forgotten sin and you may if you so desire include other sins committed since your bad confession.

It is true that certain missioners in the past have disturbed the peace of mind of the devout by hell fire and brimstone sermons on bad confessions. I have heard of such sermons upsetting whole parishes. However, these were exceptional cases and such sermons become rarer every year. It remains true, though, that missions and retreats are times of special graces and some penitents are inspired to do something about bad confessions at these times. They do not know the missioners and are more ready to bare their souls to them. In fact, this is the reason why local priests do not hear confessions during a mission.

General confessions should not be made when the repetition of the sins will only harm the penitents. This is especially true for scrupulous penitents. However, even for the scrupulous, we cannot lay down any iron-clad rules because a patient, sympathetic confessor may help a scrupulant by listening to his general confession. In the majority of cases, however, a general confession is harmful for a scrupulous person and should be allowed only when he is certain he has made bad confessions. A repetition of confession of forgiven sins may bring peace to the normal person but to the scrupulous it only increases anxiety. "Scrupulous penitents," says St. Alphonsus, "would go on making and repeating general confessions forever in the hope of laying aside their anxiety but the evil only grows, for after every general confession they fall again into new anxieties and scruples, thinking they have omitted some sin or failed to confess it properly so that their uneasiness increases the oftener they repeat their confessions."[1]

So before deciding to make a general confession, first ask

[1] Quoted by Rev. Caspar E. Schieler, *Theory and Practice of the Confessional* (New York: Benziger, 1906), p. 236.

yourself why you want to make the general confession. Is it merely that you have never made one before? That would not be a good reason. If you have heard a sermon about bad confessions and are vaguely disturbed but can find no specific reason for being worried, then don't make a general confession. If, on the other hand, you honestly feel that a general confession can help you greatly in straightening out your life and conduct, then you can make a general confession. Repetition of past confessions is *necessary* only when you have made invalid confessions but it is *recommended* whenever you feel morally certain that it will help your spiritual life.

CHAPTER 12

BLESSING OR BURDEN?

Must confession be a burden? Some parishioners feel it is the heaviest burden our religion lays upon us and they are frequently the very persons who go to confession regularly. Why is this attitude toward confession so prevalent?

In this connection, Father Scharsch says: "To make frequent confession a pleasant and profitable task, demands sound judgment and a certain facility in entering into oneself, in other words, the gift of mental concentration. There must, furthermore, be no anxiety or fear. Those who, on account of a peculiar mental disposition, find confession very difficult, assume a different attitude toward frequent confession. Some develop a direct aversion for it in consequence of the agony which they undergo. It would be wrong to urge such persons, who would profit little by frequent confession anyhow, to go every week or fortnight. They may confess their sins whenever they feel strong enough to do so. . . . It is for the confessor to judge whether it is profitable or harmful for such persons to go to confession often."[1]

He might have summarized his view by saying that lack of love makes confession seem an intolerable burden. There is no point in waiting until you "feel strong enough" to confess: it is more a matter of developing that genuine love

[1] Rev. Ph. Scharsch, O.M.I., *Confession As a Means of Spiritual Progress* (St. Louis: Herder, 1930), pp. 206–207.

of God that will make you eager and anxious to confess. There are Catholics who are strong enough in their faith but for whom confession is tiresome and tedious because it seems to be repetitious and futile. They seem to feel they could make confessions all day long without making any impression on their obstinate human nature. One woman recently said: "I violate charity, confess it every Saturday night and have the best of intentions to quit it and every Monday morning there I am back in the office retailing gossip I heard over the week end."

Now I think the trouble with such a person is that there is fear but little or no love. The person may be making his regular confession from a fear that is hardly more than a physical compulsion. He perhaps formed the habit of weekly confession years ago and now he feels that he must not miss that weekly confession or something will happen to him. Or it may be that his fear is somewhat more rational than that, but it is still fear and nothing more.

The theologians say that servile fear is harmful to the soul, whereas filial fear is good. Maybe his is a filial fear mixed with a cringing, servile attitude to confession that is full of vague foreboding. Perhaps he doesn't know exactly what he is afraid of and simply fears fear. All that he knows is that he is painfully aware that he violated some precept or other and he has a very uncomfortable feeling about it even though the violation was only a venial sin. He is under no obligation to confess it but he dreads his next regular confession because he knows he will be painfully reluctant to tell the sin to the priest. Maybe it's because he is aware that he doesn't really hate the sin at all but secretly likes it and the only reason why he doesn't commit it often is that this brooding fear deters him.

Whatever the reason may be, there are many penitents who approach the confessional with much fear but little love of God. We have to face up to the fact that the human heart has a choice of two loves: love of the world and love of God, and that the first is frightfully easy but the second is hard. The good things of the world are all around us, rich or entertaining or luscious, comforts and pleasures and amusements. They are visible and tangible. God, however, is invisible and to love Him requires effort. What many men do when faced with a choice of these two loves is to make a compromise. Cardinal Newman somewhere in his writings says of these men that they choose to love the world but moderate that love by acting according to a moral law for which they have no love. Their religion then becomes for them simply an interference with their enjoyment of the world but it gives them a sense of propriety and conscientiousness.

I suppose many Catholics at confession time have experienced remorse and regret without feeling any real love of God. They are conscious of their religion as a negative force that forbids sin but does not give rise to personal religion. They seem to be appeasing a force they fear and dread. Is it any wonder that their confessions become mechanical?

To derive the most profit from confession, to have a sense of its vital importance in our lives, one thing is necessary. St. Paul, in 1 Corinthians 13, says: "And I point out to you a yet more excellent way. If I should speak with the tongues of men and of angels, but do not have charity, I have become as sounding brass or a tinkling cymbal. And if I have prophecy and know all mysteries and all knowledge, and if I have all faith so as to remove mountains, yet do not have charity, I am nothing. And if I distribute all my goods to feed the poor, and if I deliver my body to be burned, yet do not have charity, it profits me nothing." Charity — love of God — is the abiding golden background against which you ought to live your spiritual life. This is the "yet more excellent way" to make your confession so that it will become a great help to you instead of remaining an empty formalism.

I do not mean to give the impression that every penitent must become a mystic achieving a high degree of divine union and living a supremely ascetical life. To demand too much spirituality of a penitent may develop in him an aversion for the very love that is so necessary. To develop love requires effort but not herculean exertion. Moreover, no priest should demand that a penitent express love of God in a particular form such as a desire for a special virtue. Reverend A. M. Henry, O.P. says: "God is patient. The priest must not expect the little grain of wheat to produce the ear all at once. He must know how to recognize the good that already exists, then indicate as well as he can the difficult and personal paths of growth in goodness. He will accept the fact that love may at first express itself in ways that only remotely resemble what his 'theology' has taught him to look for. He will remember that the law of the Christian is a law of liberty and above all a guide to liberty. He will teach souls to discover by themselves the virtuous and progressive co-operation that the Spirit of Christ demands of them."[2]

A certain amount of mysticism, however, is necessary in the Christian life. Our inner life is a participation in the life of Christ or it is nothing. Therefore to reduce Christian life to a matter of mere avoidance of sin and confession to a mere absolution from sin is absurd. Our ultimate aim in confession is to regain the life of Christ if we have lost it by mortal sin, and to increase the Christ life if we have diminished it through venial sin.

The obligation of obeying the Commandments represents only a part of our obligation as Christians. The total obligation is love of God, and obedience to the precepts of the moral law is only one way of showing this love. "If you love Me, keep My commandments." There is little danger that we will lose sight of the Ten Commandments. They

---

[2] A. M. Henry, O.P., ed., *Christ in His Sacraments* (Chicago: Fides, 1958), p. 265.

are down in our catechisms in black and white. They have been drummed into us since we were children. They are like guardrails to indicate danger and to protect us from disaster. But love of God has vast implications that are not down in black and white. Christ said that the first and greatest commandment was to love Him with all our heart and soul and mind and strength and He has not told us precisely how to do it, leaving it up to our divinely given ingenuity to devise ways and means of loving and expressing our love. At the same time, the devil tempts us to devise ways of violating love. There are so many possible ways to sin against love of God that it is impossible to make a catalogue of all sins. New sins are constantly being committed because changing conditions produce new opportunities to violate love of God. Years ago dueling was a popular sin; today it is payola; tomorrow we shall probably be hearing about new forms of mischief in outer space. In fact, St. Thomas said that sin includes any kind of turning away from God and toward creatures. Confession, therefore, should be a turning away from creatures and a turning toward God, a matter of personal friendship rather than an auditing of accounts.

The Ten Commandments about which we are so solicitous are really only the lowest limits of our obligation of love. And even they are at times hard to apply since they are so general. How are we to apply the Sixth Commandment to the changing conditions of our time? The Curé of Ars would have denounced as scandalous dresses that are considered modest by devout women today. To make a sound application of the Ten Commandments today, love as well as prudence is necessary.

In confession you examine your conscience and compare your actions with the external moral law that is found in our catechisms. But what about the inner law of love? It is a force that is "a sweet compulsion" that drives you to do God's will. If you have deliberately failed in love, should you not confess it? If you think of God's law only in the form of moral theology books, are you not taking on the mind of the Pharisees? St. Paul drew a distinction between the Mosaic law written on tablets of stone and the Christian moral law written "on the fleshly tablets of the heart." Don't think of God's law as something necessarily exterior but as something you have made interior through your love.

Perhaps some may say that this emphasis on love of God in confession is too theoretical for men and women of our era. We are living in a lawless, rebellious age and there should be more respect for all laws, whether of God or men. They may say also that love of God is too abstract and vague for practical morality. Now I don't mean to belittle law and set it over against love by way of contrast. Every jot and tittle of the moral law of God must stand. But I do insist that you will derive more benefit from your confessions if you enter the confessional aware of a loving, personal relationship between yourself and God rather than haunted by an impersonal relationship to a code of laws.

How to develop this love of God is a large question beyond the scope of this book. I might recommend, however, (1) that you receive the sacraments, especially Holy Communion, in a spirit of active co-operation with the Holy Spirit, the Spirit of Love, who comes to dwell in your soul; and (2) that you learn to love by doing. Practice love of God in your daily life by loving your neighbor. St. Gregory said that as birds fly out over the land before ascending the skies, so our love should go out to our neighbor before going up to God. If you work in the business world, remember that Karl Marx was a bad prophet when he said that class war between employer and employee is inevitable. It is not inevitable as long as there are Christian employers and employees who love their neighbors.

The whole history of Christ's denunciation of the Pharisees underscores the lesson that observance of the letter of the law is not enough. The Christian must go on from the letter to the fullness of interior perfection of which the letter of the law is only a shadow. Piers Plowman said: "Chastity without charity will be chained in hell. It is as lacking as a lamp without a light in it." Love is the fulfilling of the law.

INDEX